THE OPEN-TEXTURE OF MORAL CONCEPTS

THE OPEN-TEXTURE
OF MORAL CONCEPTS

J. M. BRENNAN

BARNES & NOBLE

BOOKS

10 East 53d St. New York 10022
(a division of Harper & Row Publishers, Inc.)

First published in Great Britain 1977 by
The Macmillan Press Ltd

Published in the U.S.A. 1977 by
HARPER & ROW PUBLISHERS, INC.
BARNES AND NOBLE IMPORT DIVISION

Printed in Great Britain

Library of Congress Cataloging in Publication Data

Brennan, J   M
    The open-texture of moral concepts.

    (New studies in practical philosophy)
    Bibliography: p.
    Includes index.
    1. Ethics. I. Title.
BJ1012.B65   1977   170   74–31826
ISBN 0–06–490656–6

Contents

Editor's Foreword   7
Preface   9

Part One: Understanding and Validity in Moral Judgement 15

1 Moral Perplexity 2 The Moral Point of View 3 The
Question of Rationality 4 'Is–Ought' 5 Decision
Procedures 6 Fact-Independence 7 The Structure of
Moral Perplexity 8 Universalisability and Moral
Concepts 9 Standards and Specifications 10 Standards
and Criteria 11 Similarity and Moral Types 12
'Murder' as a Moral Type 13 Standards of Justifica-
tion 14 Some Corollaries 15 Other Moral Concepts 16
Similarity and Validity 17 Further Arguments for the
Interpersonal Claim

Part Two: The Method of Ethical Inquiry   88

18 The Need for Method 19 The Claim Provides the
Method 20 Consistency and Deduction 21 From Form
to Matter 22 Consistency, Flexibility and Open-Texture 23 Settling Boundary Disputes 24 Open-Texture
and the Explication of Concepts 25 The Open-Texture
of Moral Terms 26 Open-Texture and Substantial
Moral Problems 27 Deciding Moral Issues

Part Three: Conclusions and Speculations   150

28 The Conditions and Implications of Consistency 29
Open-Texture and Consistency 30 Consistency and
Contradiction 31 A Matter of Belief 32 Consistency
and Rules 33 Moral and Non-Moral Beliefs 34 The
Moral Point of View and the Basis of Ethics

References   168

To Clare

Editor's Foreword

Mr Brennan here makes a contribution to the contemporary debate about the logical character of moral judgements. He sides with neither the prevailing naturalism nor non-naturalism. In his opinion both are mistaken: moral properties cannot be reduced to non-moral, and moral judgements must not be regarded as non-cognitive. There is, he contends, a moral point of view from which human action can be so understood and interpreted that deliberation about it, and judgement upon it, are seen to be cognitive and rational modes of behaviour 'with all that this implies'. The implications are drawn out systematically. Mr Brennan's contention, that moral concepts are open-textured in much the same way as empirical ones, will interest all students of modern philosophy.

University of Exeter   W. D. HUDSON

Preface

This is a study of a type of moral judgement and of the concepts which are employed in making these judgements. The kind of judgement that I have in mind is that which a person is called upon to make when he is considering a course of action and wonders whether it is right, or wrong, or whether it ought to be pursued. There are, of course, other kinds of moral judgement and concept; these will not be treated, although I think that, *mutatis mutandis*, some of the conclusions reached in this study could be applied to them as well. I do not apologise for this restriction of the subject-matter, because one must start somewhere and one can do only one thing at a time; moreover, the conclusions which are reached, if they are correct, are of sufficient substance and far-reaching importance to justify the inquiry.

The guiding question in this investigation is: Can we know whether something is right or wrong? Or, to put it another way: Can we rationally decide among incompatible moral opinions? The critical point which must be settled is whether or not there is something to be understood in ethical matters *qua* ethical, or if the cognitive possibilities are exhausted when all questions of logic and morally neutral fact have been settled.

The precedure will be to examine, by the use of concrete examples, the way people make moral judgements in order to discover what makes this practice intelligible; or, what is the same thing, to discover some of the necessary conditions for moral terms to be used sensibly. This means that I shall not start at the other end, as theorists tend to do, by trying to locate a source of moral thought either in the wants, interests or needs of people (which attempt is usually based on a theory of action) or in emotions, attitudes or decisions (usually attempted within a theory of knowledge), and by then building up a theory of moral judgement on this foundation. My procedure is based on the belief that the only plausible approach to the question of the basis of ethics is to work back towards it from a careful study of the practice of which it is the basis. Moreover, the present work will not include a demonstration that something or other is the basis of ethics, because this study does not purport to be a complete and adequate theory of morals, but only the first step in the development of such a theory.

One reason for trying to establish a foundation for ethics seems to be the belief that, since this foundation is logically the basis of all moral judgements, one cannot intelligently discuss moral judgements – let alone settle the question of their cognitivity or their capacity for rational justification – unless one establishes this first principle. However, this belief is false. The general rule is that first principles are implicit in existing systems of thought and that they can only be discovered, when they can, by a careful study of the relevant system. Indeed, proposed principles are tested against the established practice, and if they are inadequate to explain the practice, or especially if they are incompatible with it, they are rejected. To say that a discipline is cognitive if, and only if, it has a well-defined foundation is to claim that there is very little, if anything, that we can be said to know. If it be further required that this foundation be established in some universe of discourse other than itself, then there is nothing that we can know, because different universes of discourse are logically independent of each other. There is, therefore, something a bit odd in requiring that ethics should meet these standards; if philosophers were to apply the same standards to other disciplines as they apply to ethics, they would find that they were undermining everything they thought they knew.

The main conclusions which I shall try to establish can be set out as the answers to three questions:

(1)   Is there anything to be known or understood in ethical matters if all questions of logic and morally neutral fact are settled? I shall argue that there is a distinctive mode of moral understanding over and above, and irreducible to, any logical or factual considerations; indeed, that the latter are

meaningless unless the former has first been achieved.

(2) What sort of claim to validity do moral judgements make? I shall argue that implicit in the making of a moral judgement is the belief that anyone who considers the case properly ought to agree with that judgement. The claim is a universal claim on the judgements of others.

(3) Can moral disagreements be settled in principle? I shall argue that they can, and shall develop a typology of moral disagreements and show what is required for problems of each type to be resolved.

After having seen my programme, the reader will undoubtedly have detected that this study is related to the controversy of some years' standing as to whether ethics is distinguished only by its formal characteristics or whether it has a roughly specifiable content (which is sometimes called the controversy about 'naturalism' or about 'cognitivism' – and is, in essence, a very old problem indeed), and he will probably have decided which standard he thinks I am flying. Although this study is certainly related to that controversy and, to a large extent, took shape under its influence, it cannot be easily fitted into the terms of reference of the controversy; nor, especially, can it be said to take sides, for I think that both sides are fundamentally mistaken. It is true that my conclusions are closer to those of the one camp than to those of the other, but our approaches to the problem are in virtually diametric opposition. If one can say such a thing without sounding too presumptuous, I do with the fact–value problem what Kant did with the mind–world problem – turn it upside down, making the factual content consequent upon moral judgement rather than vice versa – and, in a sense, the position set out in these pages can be seen, not as taking sides in the controversy nor as calling down a curse upon both houses, but as offering a possible means of reconciliation.

Although I disagree, fundamentally, with both sides in the debate about naturalism, I shall not engage in any detailed criticism of their writings, for the following reasons: (a) The chief criticisms of each position are well-known and, so it seems to me, irrefutable. No good purpose would be served either in repeating them or in trying to make up new ones. (b) To write a balanced and fair critique of such serious writers would require a work as long as the present study, which would mean that I should be writing a different book. I have thought it more worthwhile to write this one. (c) To establish a position which is incompatible with a theory which one opposes can sometimes be the most effective criticism of that theory; and, in any case, I should have had to develop my own position in order to have the proper critical framework for showing why I think they are mistaken. (d) Finally, and most importantly, the establishment of my position does not in any sense require the prior demonstration of the falsity of any other theory.

Lest I give the impression of claiming undue originality, I hasten to acknowledge my debts to other writers. Three germinal ideas were provided by the late A. N. Prior, Julius Kovesi and Michael Polanyi, in each instance by means of a cryptic, unexplained remark. Prior wrote:

> Aristotle divides the possible subjects of inquiry and dispute into three broad sorts – 'natural', 'ethical', and 'logical'. Ethical naturalism may be broadly described as the view that 'ethical' propositions and inquiries are in the end just a sub-species of 'natural' ones. But we shall find that both those who assert this and those who deny it frequently end up by identifying ethical propositions with logical ones.[1]

Kovesi employed two vivid images to illustrate the impossibility of moving 'from a description which is not a description from the moral point of view to one which is a description from the moral point of view'. To ask how we do this, he says, is 'like asking how to make scrambled eggs out of fried eggs';[2] and he illustrates this further by saying that 'our different sorts of notions do not cross the floor of the house; in order to get to the other side they have to go back to their constituencies and be elected for the other side'.[3]

Polanyi, in the course of an elegant argument against the notion of 'value-free' social science, makes the following observation:

When we claim that an action of ours is prompted by moral motives, or else when we make moral judgments of others – as in recognizing the impartiality of a court of law – we invariably refer to moral standards *which we hold to be valid.* Our submission to a standard has universal intent. We do not prefer courts of law to be unbiased in the same sense in which we prefer a steak to be rare rather than well-done; our appeal to moral standards necessarily claims they be *right*, that is, binding on all men.[4] (His italics.)

I was immediately sure that each of these contentions – (1) ethics is autonomous; (2) there is no logical transition from statements made in terms formed from one point of view to those whose terms are differently formed; (3) to accept a moral standard is to acknowledge its universal validity – was both correct and important but, as it stood, unsatisfactory. Just what did these contentions mean? How could these notions be worked out and fitted together?

Although the main points of this study have not, so far as I know, been worked out in detail by anyone else, they are occasionally, as the reader will discover, the development of themes which have been stated by others.[5]

My greatest debt is unquestionably owed to Michael Polanyi, whose writings, encouragement and friendship over the past ten years have set me an unparalleled example; I can neither estimate the influence he has had on this work nor adequately express the acute sense of personal loss which his recent death has imparted to all his friends. Professor Basil Mitchell was the 'good shepherd' who saw me through many a difficult strait. I am immensely grateful to him and to Mr J. R. Lucas for their help and, especially, for their support of this unconventional project. I should also like to thank Professors Warner Wick, Harry Prosch, Gordon Kaufman and Erling Skorpen for many valuable comments and criticisms. But the ultimate obligation, as is so often and rightly the case, is to thank the person who has sustained me throughout – my wife.

The author and publisher thank Messrs Routledge and Kegan Paul for permission to reproduce M. Polanyi, *Personal*

Knowledge, pp. 249–50 and the Editor of *Philosophy* for permission to reproduce J. R. Lucas, 'The Lesbian Rule', *Philosophy*, xxx (1955) 109 ff.

Part One

Understanding and Validity in Moral Judgement

1. *Moral Perplexity*

People are sometimes perplexed about moral problems. They examine the features of a situation; they seek advice and engage in argument. This is something which requires explanation because perplexity results from a failure to understand, and it is not a universally held truth that moral problems are problems of the understanding. For example, J. Kemp quite clearly distinguishes moral behaviour from the manifestation of intelligence or skill. He notes that 'being brave, and knowing how to handle one's weapons, are both necessary conditions of being a good soldier', but that there is an important difference in the way we explain failures in either of these respects: 'The coward knows what to do, but does not do it; the incompetent soldier who cannot handle his weapons does not know what to do or how to do it.' [1]

On the other hand, it certainly appears as if we are seeking for understanding when we engage in ethical inquiry, as is testified by the use of such words as 'knowledge', 'belief' and 'opinion' in moral contexts. However, this common assessment could be mistaken and has, in fact, been frequently challenged, so it is worth our while to examine the phenomenon of moral perplexity in order to discover how moral problems arise, what they look like, and what this information tells us about the nature of ethical thought.

I shall describe examples of three types of difficulty, each of which is in some sense a moral problem but only one of which exhibits moral perplexity. For the sake of unity and easy comparison, the protagonist in each case is *A*, who is a doctor.

I   *A*'s hospital has only one unit of a very special kind of equipment. That equipment is being used to prolong the life of a terminal cancer patient who is already in a coma and beyond hope. A young accident victim is brought to the hospital whose life could certainly be saved with the aid of the special equipment but who will surely be lost without it. *A* is convinced that he is morally obliged to remove the equipment from the cancer patient and use it to save the young person's life. However, the cancer patient is *A*'s wife and he cannot bring himself to deprive her of the life-prolonging equipment.

II   *A* is extremely dedicated to his profession: he sees it as the working out of his moral commitments and is, therefore, conscientious in his striving to do the very best by each patient. A man comes to him who has a brain tumour and a weak heart. *A* cannot decide what is the best thing to do: to operate on the tumour and endanger the heart or to apply some form of therapy of whose efficacy he is not certain but which will not put too much strain on the patient's heart.

III   A young woman comes to *A* seeking an abortion. After examination *A* concludes that there would be absolutely no medical complications if he performs this operation. Also, he is sure that he could stretch the provisions of the Abortion Act to cover this case. However, *A* does not think that the girl's reasons for wanting an abortion are good enough. If, for example, he were in her place, he would not think that he was justified in terminating the pregnancy. But *A* is not an intolerant man; he does not wish to impose his views on others. *A* is therefore perplexed about whether or not it would be right for him to co-operate with what he thought to be wrong.

Example I is a moral problem, but it does not display moral perplexity because *A* is convinced that he knows what is the right thing to do. His situation, which represents a common enough experience, is similar to that of the cowardly soldier which Kemp used as an example. While it is possible that a problem of this nature could lead to moral perplexity – for example, many adolescents who find themselves incapable of avoiding masturbation, especially when they discover that this weakness is virtually universal, are led to question whether it is as wicked as they had been taught to believe – such a transition would make it a different kind of problem. As it stands, there is no perplexity. Although problems of this type are interesting and important in their own right, they are beside the present point and will, therefore, be set aside.

Neither is Example II, in any accurate sense, a case of moral puzzlement, even though A is not sure what is the right thing to do and even though he thinks that he is morally obliged to do what is best for his patient's welfare. His perplexity is technical, not moral, because he does not question whether or not he is obliged to provide the best medical care that he can; he is not sure what the best medical care is in this instance. That the problem is not a moral problem can be shown by two considerations. Another doctor of comparable skill might have no moral concern about his profession but be driven only by the desire to make money. He could well strive, in the present instance, to give the patient the best possible medical treatment because he sees it as the opportunity to enhance his reputation, and thus his fortune. He would be faced with the very same problem as was his ethical colleague about deciding upon the proper course of action. The second consideration is that we do not blame a conscientiously made, but mistaken medical judgement the way we do a moral failure. Thus we would not blame A if his patient dies despite all his efforts the way we would if, for example, A had postponed the operation because he wanted to play golf and the patient died in the meantime.

Example III is a case of moral perplexity. A does not know what he ought to do, but his confusion is not medical, legal or prudential; it is moral. This case is similar to an example used by R. M. Hare about a man who is being advised by two tax experts about a proposed attempt at tax evasion.[2] In the example, the two experts agree that what the man proposes would be legally justified, but they disagree about whether it would be morally right. That is to say, there is perplexity, but it is not legal nor, presuming that the man has normal attitudes towards money, is it prudential.

2. The Moral Point of View

The moral and technical problems exhibited in Examples II and III are clearly different types of problem, and it is worth comparing them in order to see just how they do differ.

As a first step, it is important and instructive to see the ways in which they do not differ. Both are practical problems; an answer is sought to the question: What shall I do? – or better: What ought I to do? This answer, when it is found, is an action-guiding judgement. As is characteristic of practical problems, there is in each instance an infinity of possibly relevant circumstances and consequences to be taken into account, so that the solutions are inevitably uncertain to some extent. A further characteristic of practical problems is the well-known incommensurability of thought and action which Polanyi illustrates with the following example:

> Suppose you hammer in a nail. Before starting, you look at the hammer, the nail and the board into which you will drive it; the result is knowledge which you can put into words. Then you hammer in the nail. The result is a deed; something is now firmly nailed on. Of this you can have knowledge, but it is not itself knowledge. It is a material change which counts as an achievement.[3]

He goes on to say that this performance requires the conception of a hammer, 'which defines a class of objects that are (actual or potential) hammers',[4] but that this conception is not a piece of detached knowledge. 'The suitability of an object to serve as a hammer is an observable property, but it can be observed only within the framework defined by the performance it is supposed to serve.[5] This gap between theoretical and practical knowledge is reflected in the famous logical gap between 'is' and 'ought', for the normative judgements which mediate the transition from detached knowledge to action are not of the same logical character as the judgements of what is the case.

It is important to realise that moral and technical problems have a lot in common if we are to avoid the error of supposing that the characteristics of practical problems in general are somehow special features of moral problems. But it is no less important, of course, that we discover what it is that makes them different. The clear and important difference between moral and technical judgements is that they are concerned with different things; they deal with different aspects of human behaviour; different considerations are considered relevant and important. The best evidence for this is that, in Example 11, if A were seeking advice he would surely go to someone who was a highly competent doctor, even one with whose moral views he disagreed, whereas if he sought advice in Example 111, he might go to his wife, his friend, a priest or even a moral philosopher – medical knowledge would not be required since *ex hypothesi* there are no medical complications.

I shall follow common usage and call this kind of difference a difference in *point of view*. It is possible, but not completely reasonable, to object that the notion of a point of view is not clearly enough defined to be of use in making philosophical distinctions. Such an objection is not reasonable because 'point of view' is an expression which is not only commonly used, but quite easy to understand, and I am using it in its straightforward sense. It is, of course, by analogy with visual perception that we speak of a conceptual point of view, but then a good number of the words we use to describe mental activity are similarly analogous. Furthermore, it would be difficult to define point of view without using words like 'aspect', 'respects' or 'perspective', which share the same defect.

In any case, one can clearly illustrate what is meant by difference in point of view. For example, a clever theft is an action which is appraised favourably from the technical point of view and unfavourably from the moral point of view. In Example 111 the abortion was acceptable from the medical point of view and from the logical point of view – we could give it a strong prudential appeal by imagining that A is the father and that the girl threatens to go to his wife if he does not perform the abortion – but A thought it unacceptable from the moral point of view. We can assess actions from the prudential, the technical, the legal, the moral and, no doubt, many other points of view. Which is to say, in each of these cases we employ different standards, we look for different features and accord them different relevance and importance. One could perhaps speak of an 'interpretative framework' or employ the Scholastic distinction, which Anthony Kenny has recently revived,[6] between the material and the formal object; but it is doubtful that these expressions would be any more illuminating than 'point of view'.

3. *The Question of Rationality*

It has often been maintained that there is another important
difference between technical and moral problems; namely,
that the former are susceptible of a rational solution but the
latter are not. This can be illustrated quite simply by recalling
the example quoted from Polanyi. The transition from the
detached knowledge of an object with certain properties to the
practical knowledge of that object as a hammer was effected,
in his words, 'within the framework of a useful performance'.[7]
Now, it can be argued, it is just this means–end relationship
which is lacking in the case of moral judgement. The various
teleological ethical theories which have been offered in the
past are known to suffer grave logical weaknesses, the most
damaging being that the *telos* which is proposed as the ground
for moral judgements can invariably be shown to be·itself the
product of a moral judgement. Moral judgements are lacking
in the sort of independent grounding which warrants the
acknowledgement of rational technical assessments.

The question of teleology was introduced only to illustrate
the sort of argument which might be proposed to distinguish
moral judgements from others on the basis of rationality. It is
not a question which I shall take up because it raises in turn
too many other questions that are outside the scope of the present study. What was illustrated by introducing this question
is the type of argument which claims that technical or prudential judgements, although they are normative, are somehow
more closely tied to facts than are moral judgements. There
are three different expressions of such a belief, ranging from
crude to relatively sophisticated versions. The treatment of
these will be brief because I believe that the picture of moral
judgement and inquiry which will emerge in the course of this
study will be the best evidence that the sort of argument in
question is misplaced.

4. 'Is–Ought'

The blunt expression of this type of argument is that summed up in the dictum, 'One cannot derive an "ought" from an "is" ', which received its classical expression in the famous passage in Hume's *Treatise*.[8] What is truly surprising is that this argument has been accorded such importance, for two things that we look for in assessing a philosophical argument are logical cogency and serious implications, and the value of this argument is, to say the least, questionable on both grounds.

J. R. Searle, for example, attacks the logical status of the argument, finding it ironic that 'the very terminology in which the thesis is expressed – the terminology of entailment, meaning, and validity – presupposes the falsity of the thesis'.[9] But even if we let the logical status of the 'is–ought' argument pass, we are confronted with the more damaging question of the importance of its implications. Just what does the argument prove? If the dictum that one cannot derive an 'ought' from an 'is' is taken to express a logical impossibility, then it is the mere statement of the tautology that statements which cannot be derived from statements containing 'is' cannot be derived from statements containing 'is'. Prior has complained of the tendency of philosophers to 'end up by identifying ethical propositions with logical ones' and has warned that this is to reduce one's thesis to a tautology: 'To represent an opponent's position in such a way as to make it not only false but self-contradictory is a dialectical triumph which can never be obtained without being duly paid for; and the price is the representation of one's own position as not only true but a truism.'[10]

Of course, a truism is still true for all that, and could be of value in combination with other premisses. For example, if it could be shown that the only alternatives open to us were either to believe that we could make a strict, formal derivation of moral judgements from morally neutral premisses (which *ex hypothesi* is logically impossible) or to accept the fact that no moral opinion can be preferred on rational grounds to any other, then we should be obliged to accept the latter. However, this disjunctive premiss, far from being a truism, is false. It will be one of the major tasks of the present study to show that this is not an exclusive disjunction, but even before these arguments are elaborated we can see that it is obvious that the disjunctive premiss (however important a role it has played as a presupposition of anti-naturalistic moral philosophers) is false.

It is worth recalling, as Kemp has mentioned,[11] the similarity in Hume's language when he compares empirical with logical reasoning and when he contrasts moral belief to both. One cannot formally deduce that hitting oneself on the head with a hammer is the cause of one's headache. Are there, therefore, no rational grounds for supposing that putting down the hammer will ease the pain? One cannot formally deduce a general law from the observation of individual happenings. Are there, therefore, no rational grounds for accepting the law of gravity? There are, of course, philosophers who accept the full rigour of such conclusions, but that is beside the present point. If science and common sense are both non-cognitive, then it is not saying anything distinctive about moral judgements to state that they are too.

5. *Decision Procedures*

The 'is–ought' argument is a blunt philosophical instrument because it is based on a simplistic, if not fallacious, logic and because it either proves nothing or it proves so much that it says nothing special about ethics. However, the same principle can be presented in a more refined fashion by introducing the notion of 'decision procedures'. Moral problems are said to be in principle undecidable because there are no definite procedures whereby the correct solution can be identified. I shall treat the question of the decidability of moral problems at some length in Part Two. For now, let us look at this question of decision *procedure*.

It is clear, in the first place, that a strict interpretation of the notion – as, for example, was exhibited in the use of the verification principle in the first edition of *Language, Truth and Logic*[12] – amounts to nothing more than a rewording of the argument already dismissed as too blunt an instrument. Further, it is also clear that to the degree that there is a possibility of substantial argument within a discipline there are no strict decision procedures within that discipline. This is true of disciplines which could be thought of as akin to morals, such as history, anthropology and law. It would also appear to be true of the natural sciences. If there were clearcut decision procedures in science, why did the 'spontaneous generation' controversy drag on for forty years, and why did Max Planck say that the only way to ensure that quantum mechanics would be universally accepted over classical mechanics was to wait for all the classicists to die?

Probably the most famous, and surely the most plausible, decision procedure to be proposed for science is Popper's principle of falsifiability. Its value lies in its avoidance of the logical pitfalls which ensnare both inductionist and verificationist theories. While it does not allow for the establishment of the truth of a theory, it does provide a method for a rational choice between competing theories by eliminating the falsified. Popper's theory has been under attack on general grounds by a number of philosophers, notably Kuhn and Polanyi,[13] but the most valuable critique for our present purpose has been produced from within the Popperian camp by the late Imre Lakatos.[14]

In order to demonstrate the weakness in Popper's theory, Lakatos imagines a straightforward scientific experiment: 'Let us imagine that a big radio-star is discovered with a system of radio-star satellites orbiting it. We should like to test some gravitational theory on this planetary system – a matter of some interest. Now let us imagine that Jodrell Bank succeeds in providing a set of space–time co-ordinates of the planets which is inconsistent with the theory.'[15]

This is a classical hypothetico-deductive situation. The theory has been 'falsified'. However, Lakatos points out that the experimental technique was based on the theory of radio-optics (and he shows that this is no different in principle from other experimental techniques such as Gallileo's 'observation' of Jupiter's planets), which theory is being accepted uncritically as 'background knowledge'; and he asks why this experiment should be thought of as overthrowing the gravitational theory rather than the theory of radio-optics.[16] After an extended argument which shows that there is no logical reason to distinguish between 'explanatory' theories, which are supposed to be judged by the facts, and 'interpretive' theories, which are accepted uncritically as 'unproblematic background knowledge and which are believed to yield the 'facts', he concludes: '. . . it is not that we propose a theory and Nature may shout NO. Rather, we propose a maze of theories and Nature may shout INCONSISTENT.'[17]

Thus Lakatos has convincingly argued that there are no experimental decision procedures in the natural sciences, at least in the straightforward sense that such a procedure would enable us to settle even the falsity of a theory by the application of experimental techniques.

The notion of decision procedure is especially at home within the formal disciplines, but even there only to a limited degree and in the solving of routine problems. There were no decision procedures by which to test the acceptability of Descartes's algebraisation of geometry or of Cantor's notion of non-denumerability. In even a moderately rich system, such as the Russell–Whitehead axiomatisation of arithmetic, it is possible to produce well-formed propositions which cannot be decided within the system. This has been demonstrated by Gödel's famous theorem,[18] the implications of which are even more far-reaching, for if we can demonstrate neither the completeness nor the consistency of our axioms, then the decidability of all the theorems within the system is thrown into doubt.

Thus, the lack of strict decision procedures in ethics is not a good reason for setting that discipline off from others which are thought to be more rational.

6. Fact-Independence

A third version of the argument that moral judgements are distinguished from other types is more plausible because it avoids the simplistic presuppositions of the previous two. It says that a moral judgement (as is called for in Example III above) is logically different from a technical judgement (as called for in Example II) because two people could be in complete agreement about all factual matters and still disagree in their moral judgement, whereas this could not happen in the other case.

We can borrow Hare's example in order to illustrate this: 'Let us suppose that two people know all about the income tax laws, and know, specifically, that a certain method of tax avoidance is perfectly legal; and let us suppose that they know all about the precise tax situation of somebody who is proposing to use this means of avoiding tax.' [19] Hare goes on to imagine that the two experts, with all their factual agreement, still disagree about the morality of this particular attempt at tax avoidance. This is the sort of case which would appear to substantiate the belief that moral judgements are in a special way independent of factual considerations, for a brief reflection upon the nature of the argument will reveal that no further factual considerations will be of any avail in swaying the opinion of one or the other of the disputants.

Let us codify the range of factual agreement as $a, b, \ldots n$; and call the disputants X and Y. Now if X wants to press the argument further, he will point out to Y that he thinks, say, that the course of action is justified because of d, f and h. But the difficulty is, of course, that Y has already agreed upon d, f and h, and has taken them into account in forming his opinion; therefore he cannot be persuaded to change his opinion by an appeal to these facts. The difference between this situation and that which would be produced by a dispute about Example II is readily apparent. Suppose that A calls in consultant B and that they both agree upon the basic facts about the patient but that A decides that he ought to operate because he thinks that, with proper care, the patient's heart will hold up and that B disagrees because he is convinced that the heart cannot stand the strain. Thus, despite an apparent agreement upon the facts, the prescriptive disagreement between the doctors reveals that there is an important factual disagreement between them concerning the relative strength of the patient's heart. One cannot imagine that the two doctors could be in complete agreement about the prognosis of the operation and still disagree about its advisability.

It is no doubt possible to press this question further in order to try to establish whether or not disagreements in medical assessment can always be traced to factual disagreements, but

I shall let that point pass and turn to some general and more important considerations raised by the above comparison. The assumption underlying the type of argument we are considering seems to be that one cannot rationally decide between two incompatible opinions unless one can trace the conflict to some disagreement about what the facts are. Even if we do not subject the notion of 'fact' to a deeper scrutiny (perhaps along the line followed by Lakatos), we can see that there is something very wrong about this assumption.

An illuminating example is provided by J. A. Passmore in his discussion of objectivity. He refers to an interpretation which he had written of the philosophy of Hume as a counter-example to the contention that the measure of the objectivity of a statement is its usefulness in enabling us to predict future facts.[20] For our present purpose, we can note that an interpretation of this sort stands to the text in a manner similar to the relation of a moral judgement to morally neutral facts. Differences in interpretation do not imply disagreement about interpretation-neutral facts, that is, about the words of the text. It is true that misinterpretations can sometimes be corrected by means of greater factual accuracy (e. g., by the discovery of unpublished texts or by the adjudication of variant readings), just as moral judgements can be refuted by showing that they are based on factual error, but this is not necessarily the case. It is possible that two people might have memorised every word written by Hume and yet disagree in their interpretation of Hume, as happens in the case of the Bible. Passmore thought that his interpretation of the philosophy of Hume was justified because it resolved his puzzlement about the meaning of some passages which he had previously found obscure.[21] An interpretation is valid, not because it adds new words to the text, but because it helps us to understand the words of the text. It is, analogously, not a good criticism of the rationality of ethics to point out in the manner of Hume and Ayer that moral judgements do not predicate any additional morally neutral properties of an action.

Passmore's contention that his interpretation of Hume enabled him to see previously obscure passages in a new light is paralleled by William Whewell's classical description of scientific discovery: 'To hit upon the right conception is a difficult step; and when this step is once made, the facts assume a different aspect from what they had before; that done, they are seen in a new point of view.' [22] This reminds us that it is not the case that, even in the natural sciences, all disagreements are traceable to disagreements about the facts. They are sometimes disagreements about what the facts amount to; i. e., about the interpretation of the agreed facts. One need only scan the writings of such philosophers of science as Kuhn, Pantin, Polanyi or Toulmin[23] to find ample evidence of the importance of conceptual revision. As a startling example, the Theory of Relativity, on the authority of Einstein himself, was based on no new experimental evidence but upon the very facts which were already well-known to scientists.[24]

I do not intend to become involved in controversial topics in the philosophy of science, and I have raised this question chiefly because it suggests an interesting line of inquiry which I shall take up in the next paragraph. However, even a cursory knowledge of the current literature in the philosophy of science is sufficient to justify one in questioning whether all scientific disputes can be traced to factual disagreements. While it is true that it would be wrong of me to expect that my readers should accept uncritically the views of the philosophers I have mentioned, and other like them, it is equally true that those who disagree with my position should not expect me to accept, uncritically, a positivistic philosophy of science. *Lex dubia non obligat.* If it could be shown that scientific discoveries are conceptual innovations; or, to put it another way, if it could be shown that scientific explanation is an interpretation or, as Pantin argues, a correct classification (i. e., a taxonomy) of phenomena, then it would be perfectly possible for there to be scientific disagreement where there is no disagreement about what the facts are. I shall not speculate about what this would mean to the theory of science, but it would completely break down the attempt we are considering to distinguish ethics from other disciplines. In any case, it is important that the moral philosopher examine his presuppositions, for it is not a commendatory feature of a moral theory that it be based upon an outdated or unargued theory of science.

The foregoing considerations suggest the need for another look at the way our problem has been set out, for no provision was made for the phenomenon described by Passmore and Whewell of the facts assuming 'a different aspect from what they had before'. If we think of the 'facts of a case' as a list, a, b, ... n, we get the impression of a class of things which, however they might differ among themselves, are still alike in that they are simply 'facts' – all on the same level, equally neutral, equally relevant, equally important. If we then think of two people contemplating this array of neutral facts and of one of them pronouncing that something is 'right' while the other pronounces that it is 'wrong', we are indeed at a loss to think of any sensible way of choosing between these opinions. What seems even more baffling is why the two men felt compelled to make their pronouncements at all! However, it is obvious that this picture of the lonely moral agent set over against a one-levelled, neutral array of facts and pronouncing upon them is not even a caricature of the way we actually experience the making of moral judgements; it is at best a theoretical model, and a model, one might suggest, that we would do well to compare with the actuality which it purports to illuminate.

An instructive comparison can be made with medical judgement. There is no limit to the number of correct factual statements that could be made about a given medical case. However, a doctor does not bestow an equal regard upon all these facts. Not all facts are symptoms. The step from neutral fact to medical prescription is mediated by the diagnosis which transforms the neutral array of facts into a field which is charged with significance. Some of the facts stand out as symptoms; they are accorded relevance and importance and, if they can be fused into a significant pattern, the diagnosis is complete and the appropriate prescription warranted. This parallels Polanyi's observation, which was quoted earlier, that the transition from a detached knowledge of an object with observable properties to a practical knowledge of that object as useful for hammering a nail is achieved within the framework of a useful performance. However, as we can now see, the teleological implications of Polanyi's statement were accidental; i. e., they were contingent upon the fact that he was describing a technical operation. A medical diagnosis is not assessed in teleological terms. Even though doctors generally diagnose as a means towards making a correct prescription, a diagnosis would still be correct whether or not it was relied upon to make a prescription; e. g., if it were made by a medical student in a test. Therefore, we can generalise Polanyi's statement to say that any features of an object (in the broad sense) are significant only within a given context of meaning. Or, as Whewell expressed it: 'the facts assume a different aspect from what they had before; that done, they are seen in a new point of view'.

Is there anything in moral behaviour which corresponds to the medical diagnosis? Let us expand our example of the tax experts to see if there is any evidence of this: The man whose tax situation is in question is an artist of some sort. His income is sporadic because it depends upon the sale of his creations, and let us suppose that each sale brings him a great deal of money but that it takes him several years to complete a book, or a composition, or whatever it is. It happens that he has just made a big sale, and he has discovered a legal loophole whereby he can give a substantial portion of his income to his wife as a tax-free gift. The two experts know all about this and agree that he can get away with it in law, but they dispute about the morality of it. The one says that, since it is unfair to tax people like this on the same basis as people who earn regular yearly incomes, the artist is justified in seeking a means of redress which will make his tax share equitable. The other maintains that, since his 'gift' will come right back to him for his own use, he is violating the spirit of the law, and his action is therefore dishonest and wrong.

This is all quite comprehensible, but how does it accord with our picture of an array of neutral facts? Imagine how odd it would sound if one adviser had said: 'I think that he is absolutely wrong to do this because, over a period of time, his income will be taxed at a much higher rate than that of others who earn the same amount.' Or if the other said: 'He is perfectly justified in doing this. After all, the money he gives his wife will come right back to him for his own use.' It is not the case, that is to say, that the contrary moral opinions were based upon the same facts; they were based on quite different facts. The men did not say that, because of $a, b, \ldots n$, the action was right or wrong, as the case may be. Clearly, they would have ignored most of the facts as irrelevant, and one could share their surprise if the advisee had said: 'I don't know what you two are talking about; I thought it was all right because my wife's name is Mary.' Even though his wife's name is as much a fact as those which his advisers deemed important, we recognise that his suggestion is as absurd as would be a doctor's statement that he thinks the operation will be successful because the patient's name is John.

In other words, the suggestion that people could form contrary moral opinions although they were in complete factual agreement is misleading, because to say that so-and-so is the case is not the same as to say that so-and-so is relevant or important, and moral judgements are based on the facts which are relevant and important. We need to recognise a diagnostic phase in ethical inquiry because it is only when certain facts become charged with moral significance that we become aware that a moral judgement or decision is called for; just as it is only when certain facts are recognised as symptoms that we become aware of the need for medical treatment. Any theory which suggests that we leap from a survey of neutral facts to a moral prescription that something is right, or wrong, or ought to be done, is inadequate, because an adequate theory of moral judgement must account for the fact that only some considerations are relevant and important. To put it another way, we cannot understand moral judgements until we realise that such judgements are comprehensible only within a context of meaning which bestows significance upon certain features of a situation and thus lifts them out of the background of 'neutral fact'.

It might be objected that I have relied too heavily upon common sense in my interpretation of the tax case, because, while it is true that most of us would think it odd if the men were to say the words I put into their mouths, this is only because the opinions they expressed go against our own moral preconceptions. Logically, the objection would go, there is no reason why two people might not form contrary moral opinions based on the very same fact.

In an obvious sense, this is to beg the question, for we are trying to discover whether moral opinions are, in some distinctive way, independent of factual considerations, and it will not do simply to assert that they are. Alasdair MacIntyre, referring to C. L. Stevenson's conclusion that moral disagreements are in principle interminable, comments: 'It is not surprising that this should be a consequence of Stevenson's position, since he himself initially laid it down as one of the prerequisites for a successful theory that it should provide for disagreement to be interminable.'[25] Similarly, the present objection is taking as a starting-point precisely that proposition whose value we are investigating.

If what is meant is that, given any neutral catalogue of facts, there is no contradiction in terms involved in combining this list with a normative word like 'right', 'wrong' or 'ought', then this is perfectly true, since it is merely a truism. Given any finite series of events, there are an infinite number of possible explanations; therefore, the probability of any scientific theory is zero; therefore, there is no contradiction of terms involved in combining this list of facts with any of an infinite number of theories.

The quest for logical consistency makes sense only within a given context of meaning. Terms formed from one point of view (e. g., colour words) cannot be in contradiction with terms formed from another point of view (e. g., shape words or physical-object words). Therefore, to say that a list of neutral facts cannot contradict a normative statement is to say next to nothing. What I tried to show by the tax example – a point which will be elaborated at length throughout the remainder of this study – is that moral judgement is not the pinning of a normative label upon a uni-levelled, neutral array of facts, but that moral questions arise only within a structured situation. The sort of detached logic which is employed in the objection is worthless as a critical tool – not only with regard to moral discourse, but with regard also to any structured discourse, including that of science – because it does not take account of the context of meaning within which the terms are being used and within which inferences are being drawn.

The arguments of the preceding pages do not purport to prove that we can rationally decide between contrary moral opinions. This is a topic for investigation – not a matter for postulation – and, further, the whole of the present study will claim no more than to have laid some of the groundwork for an adequate treatment of the problem. But before any progress can reasonably be hoped for, we must be quite clear about the topic we are investigating. For example, the most puzzling feature of the model of moral judgement which we have just been considering (which is that characterised by Iris Murdoch as the 'current view of morality')[26] is that anyone should feel inclined to make moral judgements at all. If all facts are equally neutral, equally devoid of moral significance, then it is difficult to see how any factual situation could ever suggest a moral problem and, therefore, why there should be any occasion to wonder whether something is right or wrong. That people are sometimes perplexed by moral problems is, as I have mentioned, a fact which requires explanation.

7. *The Structure of Moral Perplexity*

In his discussion of the structure of practical problems, of which moral problems are a sub-class, D. P. Gauthier shows that practical judgements stand to practical problems as answer to question.[27] Since we cannot make sense out of an answer, let alone assess its correctness, unless we know the question to which it is the response, a necessary step to an understanding of moral judgements is an understanding of the problems which prompt them.

In the discussion which follows, I shall be relying upon the common standards of the society of which I am a member in order to identify moral problems. The discussion will not thereby suffer from a lack of generality, because the object of my study is not the correctness of the standards, but the manner in which they are employed. The conclusions which are reached will apply equally to people with different standards because the logical structure which is uncovered is not dependent upon content, just as the logical structure of our use of 'murder' does not differ from that of 'stealing' and as the logical structure of our use of 'red' does not differ from that of 'green' even though the respective members of each of these pairs differ from the others in content.

A detached point of view is not possible in the discussion of this question (if it is ever possible) for the simple reason that there are no moral problems *per se*. Problems do not exist independently of perplexed people, and what is a problem to one person is not always a problem to another. We find moral problems when we find people in doubt about whether a course of action is right or wrong; so if we want to understand moral problems, we must find out why people are perplexed about what is right or wrong.

Let us suppose that a modern David were to approach us for advice, wondering whether it would be right or wrong for him to send Uriah into battle. We would know what he was talking about and how to go about answering him, since such an action seems tantamount to murder. But if someone is perplexed about whether he would be right or wrong to buy a new car or to take a walk by the sea, we would be at a loss as to how to advise him until we knew why he thought there was a problem. People are not perplexed about what is right or wrong unless they think that there is some reason for saying that something is right or wrong. If, upon questioning, our inquirer were to explain that he was worried that buying a new car was an unjustified extravagance in the face of world poverty, or that he thought that it might be wrong for him to take a walk because he was expecting a telephone call on a matter of great urgency to several people, we would feel at home and be able to discuss the problem intelligently, because we could see the reason for his perplexity.

When we judge that an action is right or wrong, we do this by applying a moral standard. Similarly, when we wonder whether an action is right or wrong, we are wondering about the applicability of a moral standard. Where there is no apparent relationship to any moral standard – for example, when an act is described as 'taking a walk by the sea' – the question of rightness or wrongness does not arise. But if the same physical action is seen under the description 'possible neglect of a serious duty', a new aspect emerges, the scene is charged with moral significance, and we are alerted to the presence of a moral problem and the need for moral judgement and decision.

In general, we can say that a situation is morally

problematic when the agent suspects that a proposed course of action is one which is governed by a moral standard which he holds. Now, as Hare has pointed out, the acceptance of a standard has a covert universality because the standard must apply to all similar cases.[28] Therefore, we can transpose the above definition to say that a moral problem is the question whether an action is of a type which is governed by an accepted moral standard.

It follows from this that, in the absence of moral standards, there are no moral problems, and that what is a moral problem to one person (say, an orthodox Roman Catholic) might not be a problem to someone else who holds different standards (say, a dedicated member of the Family Planning Association). It also follows from this that our moral standards define classes of actions formed from the point of view of moral rightness (that is, all the members of the class require the same judgement of rightness or wrongness). This is the basis of the 'principle of universalisability'.

Since the definition of classes of morally appropriate or inappropriate actions is a type of concept-formation, I shall call these classifications 'moral concepts' and the terms which designate them, where we have such terms, as 'moral terms'. It is a contingent fact that only some of these concepts are designated by terms. For this reason, I shall, when it will not be misleading to do so, take the concepts so designated as typical examples with the understanding that what is said about them can also be said about all the concepts under discussion. There are, of course, many moral concepts which perform functions other than the classification of actions from the point of view of their rightness. Needless to say, the present discussion cannot be applied to them without appropriate modifications. The moral terms which I am investigating would appear to be what Eric D'Arcy calls 'moral species terms.'[29]

Moral concepts play a diagnostic role in ethical inquiry, since it is through their agency that a neutral array of facts – which are neither relevant nor irrelevant, but meaningless – are transformed into a field charged with significance. Or, if you will, it is by means of our moral concepts that we recognise certain factual features as moral symptoms and accord them relevance and importance. Moral inquiry is like scientific inquiry in which the collection and assessment of facts is carried out with reference to some hypothesis. The hypothesis in a moral inquiry is that a course of action is right or wrong because it is a member of a class of actions governed by a moral concept, and a moral judgement is the judgement that this is, or is not, the case. A moral judgement, then, is not the intonation of 'right' or 'wrong' over an array of neutral facts. It is the answer to a question which is raised only within a situation which has been structured by a moral concept, and it is of the form: 'Yes, this is wrong because it is a murder.'

8. Universalisability and Moral Concepts

In our discovery of the indispensable role of moral concepts in the recognition of moral problems, we noticed that these concepts define classes − or, if you will, that moral terms designate types − of action, all the members of which require the same judgement of rightness or wrongness. This is the basis of the 'principle of universalisability' which says that the judgement of what is the right course of action in a given situation commits one to the judgement that the same course of action would be right for anyone, including oneself on future occasions, who is similarly situated. In order to judge differently about two acts, one must be able to point to some differences either in what is done or in the circumstances in which it is done, or in the person who does it.

We could formulate the principle of universalisability to say that the judgement that act a is right (wrong) in situation s implies that a is a member of a class of actions A and s is a member of a class of situations S; and that, whenever we have a member of S, a member of A is the right (or wrong) action in that situation. ('Situation', of course, refers to the whole complex of objective circumstances and personal characteristics.) This judgement could be either the identification of a specimen of an already recognised class or the 'definition' (in the sense of 'establishing the limits') of a new class. An example of the first would be to say: 'That would be murder, therefore it is wrong.' An example of the second would be for one (if, indeed, there could be one) who had never heard of the old dilemma to say: 'I know that lying is wrong, but if I tell this man the truth he will kill the other. In a case like this it is right to be untruthful.' (There does not seem to be unanimity as to whether words like 'murder', 'stealing' and 'lying' are correctly used only to express moral condemnation; or whether, especially in the case of 'lying', it is also legitimate to use them in a morally neutral sense. For the sake of convenience and clarity, I shall use them only in the first sense: i.e., in the sense that it would be a contradiction to say 'justified murder'. I shall give further reasons to support this choice.)

A necessary condition for the usefulness of the principle of universalisability is that one be able to recognise the members of the appropriate class; i. e., he must be able to tell which cases are similar in the relevant aspects. This is the function of our moral concepts. I want to inquire now into the logical structure of these concepts in order to see what is required if they are to provide the basis for universalisation.

One clue to a possible explanation is provided by a closer inspection of the principle of universalisability. It is based on the logical principle that differing moral appraisals imply some other difference among the cases so judged. Thus, if we are at a loss to tell what makes cases similar, we at least know that, when they are not similar, this dissimilarity can be expressed in 'factual' (i. e., morally neutral) terms. It is tempting to go on to say that, if dissimilarity can be expressed in factual terms, then so can similarity; and if this is so, then universalisability is no more than a function of the meanings of the factual terms employed. To use the symbols which have been introduced, a and s can be described in morally neutral terms, and by A and S we mean anything that can be described in these same terms. This would appear to provide the classifications which are needed in order to judge like cases alike.

The first thing to notice about the proffered explanation is that is is not entailed by the requirement for logical consistency. That a difference in moral assessment implies that the two cases are different in some other respect does not entail that a similarity in moral assessment implies a similarity in some other respect. We can see this by considering a non-moral example which is sometimes used to illustrate the requirement of logical consistency. I cannot say of two identical prints that one is a good picture but that the other is not, because they look exactly alike. But this does not imply that all pictures that I say are good must look exactly alike! In fact, a very poor copy of a great painting looks more like the original than does another great painting.

When we say that an agent cannot, without inconsistency, assess two cases differently unless he can point to some morally neutral differences between them, we mean that this difference must be something that another could recognise without any reference to the agent's moral standards. For example, if someone wants to say that there is a moral difference between putting a person in a gas chamber because he is a Jew and putting a person in a gas chamber because he is a convicted murderer, he can point to the difference between 'being a Jew' and 'being a convicted murderer', which difference can be understood by others who do not know his moral standards. This is not, of course, to say that this difference has nothing to do with the agent's moral standards; it obviously is a clue to them, since the agent considers it to be a morally relevant distinction. When we say that the difference is morally neutral we do not mean that it is morally irrelevant, but that the difference can be detected without understanding its relevance.

Similarity between cases is clearly not morally neutral in this sense, because unless one sees the relevance of certain features in different cases one cannot see that they are similar cases. Shooting a man in order to marry his wife is, in many respects, like shooting a man in a hunting accident or shooting a man who is shooting at you and, in these respects, quite unlike poisoning someone in order to inherit his money. But if one knows which respects are relevant, one knows why the first and last are cases of murder and why they are similar to putting a person in a gas chamber because he is a Jew. 'Relevance' is not an absolute term; something which is 'relevant' must be 'relevant *to*' something else. In the present instance, 'relevant respects' means 'respects which are relevant to the classification of certain acts as murders'; but this relevance is determined by the definition of 'murder'. If one wants to say that some acts are wrong because they are murders, one is saying that to know why they are similar is the same as to know why they are wrong.

Thus, we cannot say that like cases are alike in a morally neutral way if we mean by this that someone could tell which cases are alike without any reference to the moral standards by which they are being judged, since the standards determine which respects are relevant. A moral concept, then, is not the classification of actions which are similar in accordance with a morally neutral description, but in accordance with a morally relevant description; that is, they are similar because they are all judged to be right or wrong by appealing to the same standard. To refer to a standard for saying that some act is right or wrong is to give the reason for saying that it is right or wrong; for example, poisoning someone in order to inherit his money is wrong because it is murder. Therefore, we can define a moral concept as *the classification of actions which are judged to be right or wrong for the same reason.*

It perhaps sounds strange to say that actions are similar only because they are right or wrong for the same reason, and, indeed, this proposition has some serious implications. Nevertheless, it is what we should expect if we give a little thought to the notion of universalisability. Since there is no limit to the number of correct descriptions which could be applied to any given action, and since each of these descriptions defines a class of similar actions, there is no way to tell, from the detached point of view, which type of action the moral agent is committed about when he judges that something is right or wrong. One must know under what description the judgement was made; which is to say, one must know which features of the case the agent had in mind when he decided that the action was right or wrong. Now, if we were to ask someone who had just made a moral judgement why he decided it the way he did, he might be expected to answer that, because of such-and-such feature, or features, of the case, he thought that what he had decided was right. This is, in an obvious sense, to give a reason for saying that an action is right or wrong, and, in this sense, there is no doubt but that like cases are alike because they are right or wrong for the same reason, since this is to say no more than that they are alike in the relevant respects.

If we were to press our moral agent further and ask him why he based his decision on these features of the case and not on any of the others, he would try to show us that the other features are irrelevant – or, if relevant, of less importance. Since a morally neutral description *qua* morally neutral provides no clue as to what is morally relevant or important, this discrimination can be effected only in the light of a moral standard. Thus, the presence of the appropriate features is the reason for the judgement of rightness only in a secondary sense, since the moral standard determines their appropriateness and is, therefore, the reason for saying that their presence warrants the judgement. Let us be quite clear about what is implied by this. Since it is only if one knows the appropriate moral standard that one can tell what counts as an action of a certain type, the similarity between these actions cannot be detected without a prior grasp of the moral standard. This means that a moral term cannot be defined in morally neutral terms; or, to be more precise, it means that no morally neutral description will be able to denote all and only those actions denoted by a moral term. Before developing this thesis at length, I shall attempt to clear up a few *a priori* difficulties.

9. *Standards and Specifications*

The contention that we can tell which cases are alike only if we know the moral standard by which they are being judged might appear to say nothing more than that we do not know what types of action a person approves or disapproves of unless we know his moral standards. This is something like saying that a chef does not know how to cook the customer's steak until he knows how the customer likes it, or that a traveller does not know on which side of the road to drive in a foreign country until he knows what policy has been adopted in that country. Clearly, in these examples, anyone who understands the meaning of, say, 'rare' or 'left side' knows how to follow the instructions and, analogously, if we know that someone thinks that a certain type of action – let us call it 'so-and-so' – is wrong, we need only understand the meaning of 'so-and-so' in order to tell which cases must be treated as alike in this regard.

There is an ambiguity in the statement that we know how to judge like cases alike if we understand the meaning of 'so-and-so', the clarification of which will help give a sharper definition to the position which I shall try to defend. The crucial question is, whether or not 'so-and-so' designates a type of action such that these actions are similar to one another regardless of our taking up a moral position concerning them, and such that people with different moral standards with regard to so-and-so's would still recognise this similarity, or whether 'so-and-so' designates a type of action such that an action is a so-and-so if, and only if, it is morally right or wrong, and such that people with different standards would consider different actions as so-and-so's: that is, as similar in the relevant respects.

If 'so-and-so' is taken to designate a moral type of action – as defined in the second part of the above disjunction – then the statement, 'So-and-so is wrong', is analytic; but the contention that we can tell which cases are alike only if we know the moral standard by which they are being judged, cannot be reduced to the tautology that we know what a person approves only if we know what he approves, for to know that someone disapproves of so-and-so's is not to know what he considers to be so-and-so's; we would have to know the *rationale* (or, if you will, the *logos* or logic) which he is following in his identification of so-and-so's. If 'so-and-so' is, in this sense, a moral term, then one can tell why an action is a so-and-so only if one can tell why it is wrong.

On the other hand, if 'so-and-so' is taken to designate a morally neutral type of action, the situation is reversed. 'So-and-so is wrong' is not analytic, but my contention about like actions reduces this to a tautology. In this view, the question of why actions are similar is unrelated to the question of why they are wrong, just as the question of what counts as a rare steak is unrelated to the question of anyone's preference for rare steak. This requires that there be independent types of action which moral standards specify as right or wrong. In other words, a moral concept is a morally neutral classification of actions to which a moral label has been attached: i. e., the moral judgement about the rightness of a class of actions is extrinsic to the actual classifications and could be detached, leaving the class of actions intact but now morally neutralised. For example, 'murder' designates a type of action which could be identified without any reference to the question of whether it is right or wrong. Therefore, in this view, 'Murder is wrong' is a synthetic judgement. Others who did not adopt this principle could still use 'murder' correctly without being committed to the judgement that it is wrong.

I shall argue for the first view which says that moral judgement enters into the constitution of the concept, so that, if one does not know why a class of actions is right or wrong, one cannot identify the members of that class; if there were no moral judgement, there would be no class. I am saying, that is, that the types of action governed by moral standards are not independent types; the actions are similar to each other only from the moral point of view. Just as the speed of falling bodies, the orbit of Mars and our own earth-boundedness are unrelated phenomena without the concept of gravity, so are individual murders indistinguishable acts of homicide apart from the moral judgement that they are wrong. If 'murder' is taken as a moral concept, the statement 'Murder is wrong' is analytic.

I must point out that I am not dictating usage. It is immaterial to my position that the word 'murder' is sometimes used in a morally neutral sense. In America, for example, baseball crowds frequently shout: 'Murder the umpire!', clearly implying that they believe that the course of action which they recommend is perfectly justified. However, if 'murder' is used in this extended sense, then, not only is 'Murder is wrong' not analytic, but, by normal standards, false. One could say only that some murders are wrong, which means that one would have to give the criteria for distinguishing these wrongful murders from the others.

Let us call this sub-class 'murder$_1$'; then 'Murder$_1$ is wrong' is analytic. Therefore, if 'murder' is used as a moral term, as it is in the statement 'Murder is wrong', then it means what we have called 'murder$_1$', and the statement is analytic. It is true that someone who did not subscribe to the normal moral belief about murder could still use 'murder' correctly, but he would be using it in the 'inverted comma' sense to mean 'acts which others call "murder" '. (There are some rules of conduct of the form, 'So-and-so is wrong', which are considered, at least by some people, as moral rules and in which 'so-and-so' designates a morally neutral type of action: e. g., 'Pre-marital sex is wrong'. I shall discuss the status of such rules in section 15 below. Here we need only note that all that is required for my position is that *not all* moral rules are of this sort. The arguments, I think, will support a much stronger conclusion.)

It is no coincidence that the examples I used, to illustrate the position that moral standards specify morally neutral types of action as right or wrong (preference for rare steak, and the policy of driving on the left side of the road), reflect anti-naturalist, or non-cognitivist, moral theories – by which I mean those theories, generally associated with the tradition of Humean empiricism, which deny that there is anything to be known (apart from logical and factual considerations) in ethical matters and that there can be any rational justification of moral judgements.

This position, while it is not implied by, does depend upon, as a necessary condition, the interpretation of moral concepts which says that the actions classified by these concepts belong to independently identifiable types. The position is not implied because, interestingly, ethical naturalism also requires this interpretation. The drawing of moral inferences from morally neutral descriptions clearly demands the ability to identify the premisses independently of the conclusion. Thus, the naturalists and the anti-naturalists are alike in thinking that the taking of moral judgements is consequent upon the identification of morally neutral types of action; they disagree, of course, in that the naturalists think that they discern a deductive bond between the two, whereas their opponents, not believing in this bond, have had to look elsewhere – e. g., in attitudes or decisions – for the source of the moral judgement. I shall try to show that both sides in this continuing debate are mistaken because their arguments include the false premiss that the types of action designated by moral terms can be correctly described in morally neutral terms. Although the empiricist position cannot be derived from this fallacious interpretation of moral concepts without the help of other premisses concerned with the logical propriety of fact–value deductions, this interpretation is a necessary ingredient of the position since, unless there were the required independently identifiable types of action, there would be nothing to take up attitudes or to make decisions *about*.

10. Standards and Criteria

A second *a priori* difficulty is suggested by my contention that, unless there were independently identifiable types of action, there would be nothing to take up attitudes or make decisions *about*. 'That is quite true', an objector might say, 'but it is equally true that there would be nothing to make moral judgements about either.'

Let me show that this is not exactly the case by the use of a simple parallel. In order to say 'I like apples', or 'I have adopted the policy of eating an apple a day', one must be able to identify a ('preference-free' or 'decision-free') type of thing which is designated by 'apple'. However, in order to say 'This is an apple', all that is required, other things being equal, is that one understand the meaning of 'apple'; and this certainly does not require that one have made a prior identification of a type of thing which could be described in 'apple-neutral' words. To say this would be to become involved in an infinite regress, for the terms in which the neutral description is given would then require, if they were to be meaningful, that there be yet further independent types, and so on.

What I am suggesting, then, is that 'murder' is, in this respect, like 'apple': that it is a word which designates a type of thing and that the grasping of the appropriate notion enables one to identify the members of the corresponding class. 'Murder' differs from 'apple' in other respects, of course – chiefly in that the latter designates a type of fruit whereas the former designates a type of morally wrong action – but in as much as they are similar they can be treated similarly, and 'This is a murder' (like 'This is an apple' and unlike 'I like apples') can be sensibly uttered without there being a prior identification of a neutral type of action.

It would be quite reasonable to object that we must be able to say something about these moral types other than that all the members are right or wrong. Otherwise two people who are using a word like 'murder' would never be able to ascertain whether they are talking about the same sort of action or not. I shall later give reasons for saying that, in fact, people frequently are *not* talking about the same things when they use moral terms, and shall try to explain the anomaly that, in two different senses of 'mean', they agree on the meaning of the moral term but mean different things by it. Of course, we can give morally neutral descriptions of the sort of actions which we think are of a given moral type. For example, poisoning someone in order to inherit his money, shooting someone in order to steal his wife and putting someone in a gas chamber because he is a Jew are instances of 'murder'. However, it would be a mistake to think that these neutral descriptions could be exhaustive characterisations of the moral term – so that they would denote all and only those things denoted by the moral term – and it would be a worse mistake to suppose that one did not properly understand 'murder' unless one could clearly define it in morally neutral terms.

We must be wary, in the first place, of what, with due reverence, might be called the 'Socratic fallacy'; i. e., the contention that, unless one can give an airtight definition of something, one does not know what one is talking about. We can see an expression of this when, at the end of Book I of the *Republic*, Socrates chides himself for allowing Thrasymachus to divert him from his search for the definition of 'justice', 'so that now the result of our conversation is that I know nothing. For when I do not know what justice is, I am hardly likely to know whether it is a virtue or not, or whether he that possesses it is happy or unhappy.' [30]

One difficulty with this contention of Socrates's is the notorious paradox of Meno: 'Why, on what lines will you look, Socrates, for a thing of whose nature you know nothing at all? Pray, what sort of thing, amongst those that you know not, will you treat us to as the object of your search? Or even supposing, at the best, that you hit upon it, how will you know it is the thing you did not know?' [31]

Another is that the conversations in Book I of the *Republic* clearly demonstrate that Socrates *did* know the meaning of 'justice'. He was able, for example, to show the inadequacy of the definitions proposed by Polymarchus and Cephalus by choosing appropriate counter-examples and, on the other hand, he knew that their proposals, though inadequate, were the right sort of consideration because he argued against Thrasymachus that to rule out considerations of this kind was like ruling out a numerical definition of 'twelve'.[32]

The paradoxical fact that we know things which, in another sense of the word, we do not *know* presents a vexing problem to the theory of knowledge, but, for our purposes, it points to the fundamental fallacy that there is no middle ground between *episteme* and total ignorance. This underlying assumption has caused a great deal of trouble in every branch of philosophy, but nowhere, I think, more than in moral philosophy, for some philosophers seem to have said that, because moral judgements cannot be conclusively proved to be true, not only can we not be certain that we are right, but even that there is nothing to be known at all – i. e., that moral judgements are 'non-cognitive'.

In the present philosophical era, when one speaks less of truth and knowledge and more of meaning and analysis, the 'Socratic fallacy' persists in a different guise. Searle deals with it in reference to W. Quine's position in 'Two Dogmas of Empiricism'.[33] The problem is stated thus:

> It has often been suggested that we lack an adequate analysis of the concept of analyticity and consequently that we lack adequate criteria for deciding whether a statement is analytic. It is further suggested that because of this lack of analysis and criteria, we do not even properly understand the word and the very notion is illegitimate, defective, incoherent, unempirical, or the like. This form of argument – we lack analysis and criteria for a concept *C*, therefore we do not properly understand *C*, and until we can provide analysis and criteria for *C*, it is somehow or in some respects illegitimate – has frequently occurred in the writings of analytic philosophers since the war and it is worth examining in some detail.[34]

He goes on to say that the reason that a straightforward definition of 'analytic' – 'true in virtue of its meaning' – is considered unacceptable is that it depends upon the equally difficult notion of 'meaning' and that: 'What is wanted is a criterion of quite a different kind – extensional, formal, or behavioural'.[35]

Searle maintains that this sort of objection rests on 'mistaken assumptions about the relations between our understanding of a notion and our ability to provide criteria of a certain kind for its application'.[36] He demonstrates this by proposing a criterion which satisfies the requirement of formalist objectivity but which is obviously absurd – 'a statement is analytic if and only if the first word of the sentence used in making that statement begins with the letter "A" ' – and by then asking how it is that we know it is absurd.[37] The answer is obvious: we know the meaning of 'analytic' and, therefore, the sort of considerations which are relevant to deciding whether a statement is analytic and, further, we know that spelling is not a relevant consideration. 'Far from showing that we do not understand the concept of analyticity, our failure to find criteria of the proposed kind presupposes precisely that we do understand analyticity. We could not embark on our investigation if we did not understand the concept, for it is only in virtue of that understanding that we could assess the adequacy of proposed criteria.'[38] In other words, the meaning of a word and the criteria for its application are not the same thing. (In certain rare instances they might coincide – e. g., with geometric notions like 'rectangle' – but this is disputable and, anyway, irrelevant to our present study.) Our understanding of the meaning of a word is logically prior to, and a necessary condition of, our ability to choose appropriate criteria, and the meaning serves as the standard for assessing the adequacy of any proposed criterion.

It would not be difficult to buttress Searle's conclusion with a good number of examples from the writings of philosophers. I shall content myself with one brief reference which I think will make the point. In a paper entitled 'Modality and Quantification',[39] B. Rundle considers some of the difficulties attendant upon the introduction of tense- and modal-operators into quantification theory. His actual argument is not a matter of present concern, but his method of procedure illustrates the relation between meaning and (in this case, formal) criteria. Rundle considers various statements made in ordinary language (e. g., 'Napoleon was a general' and 'The first man into space might not have been a Russian'). He then offers a symbolic representation and goes on to show that the formalisation is ambiguous by retranslating the expression into two different ordinary language statements which are both possible interpretations. A correction is made by the introduction of various operators, but this, in turn, creates new ambiguities which require further adjustments of the calculus. The point – which is verified by his description of his project as 'the preservation of intuitively reasonable inferences' [40] – is that, at each step, the formal operations were performed under the guidance of, and were criticised in the light of, the informal meanings. This, I think, represents the experience of any reflective logician and is an exact parallel to the procedure which is followed in the attempt to establish extensional criteria for empirical terms – a project which Waismann demonstrated to be incapable of a final, adequate prosecution. [41]

We can profitably apply Searle's analysis to the conversations of *Republic* I. 'Truthfulness' and 'repayment of anything that we have received' are extensional criteria of the notion 'justice'. When Socrates demonstrates that they do not adequately define 'justice' [42] he is clearly relying upon his understanding of that notion in order to provide the counter-example of the mad man reclaiming his weapons. Similarly, when Thrasymachus enjoins Socrates to 'say how you define justice; and don't dare to tell me that it is the obligatory, or the expedient, or the profitable, or the lucrative, or the advantageous, but make your answer precise and accurate' [43], he could well serve as the prototype of the analytic philosopher demanding that he be provided with extensional criteria which would obviate the need for personal judgement in the designation of an act as 'just'. Socrates's reply can serve as a model, since the demand for a non-normative definition of a normative term is like requiring a non-numerical definition of twelve, and, as has been mentioned, the whole of Book I is a testimony to Socrates's knowledge of the meaning of 'justice' even though no definition, extensional or otherwise, was found.

We can get at the presuppositions of the present objection

by trying to understand why anyone might object to my saying: 'I do not know how to recognise murders unless I understand the meaning of 'murder', and since 'murder' is a moral term it is part of its meaning that it embodies a moral standard.'

Perhaps it might be thought that there is something odd about a word, or the notion it expresses, embodying a standard and at the same time having a denotation, unless its meaning is compounded of a standard *plus* a normal meaning in such a way that it is the latter which is the object of understanding and which is relied upon to identify specimens and that the role of the standard is to indicate that all the specimens so identified are to be praised or condemned, as the case may be. This, for example, is the way that emotively charged words (and, more generally, Nowell-Smith's 'Janus-words') operate, and as Russell's famous 'conjugations' show, we can get the same, or virtually the same, denotation with the use of an emotively neutral term. The confusion of moral terms with this sort of word has consumed (one is tempted to say wasted) a great many man-hours, even those of philosophers who are far from being emotivists, but it is a confusion, for this comparison highlights only a peripheral and unimportant feature of moral terms; namely that, because their subject-matter is so serious, they have become emotionally charged.

But is it so very odd to think of a word in which the embodied standard is not, as it were, appended to the normal meaning but is actually constitutive of the meaning so that it is only by relying upon the standard that one can identify the denoted instances? Consider the word 'unsafe' as used by an experienced mountaineer. It is, in the first place, a normative word and, secondly, it is a word whose applicability to various slopes, manoeuvres and equipment must be learned. It is obvious that the experienced mountain climber has not memorised a list of 'unsafe' things, which list could be expressed in safety-neutral terms, because he must constantly encounter novel physical situations, climb with new companions who employ unprecedented techniques, be offered new types of equipment, and he must be able to recognise if these are unsafe, else he would not have lived long enough to become an 'experienced' mountain climber. Part of his experience is the development of proper standards of safety, and he relies upon these standards to say that one thing or another is unsafe.

Perhaps more striking is the word 'table'. In an argument which I shall extend in Part Two (section 24), Kovesi[44] shows that, although tables are observable objects, the meaning of 'table' cannot be expressed in a list of observable properties and that the concept 'table' embodies a standard which objects must meet if they are to count as tables. It is not the case that one does not understand the meaning of 'table' unless one can give a table-neutral description which will denote all and only those things denoted by 'table', not only because such a list cannot be exhaustive, but chiefly because it is precisely by one's understanding of what it is to be a table that one knows what sort of properties to look for in tables.

If we return to our objection, we can see at once that it is based on the presupposition that to understand the meaning of a term is the same as to know the criteria for its application, and we have seen that this is a mistake since one must understand the meaning before one can begin to consider criteria. Much more importantly, the objection contains a breathtaking *petitio principii*. Why should it be thought that we can understand words like 'unsafe' (and, therefore, an indefinite number of similar words) and 'table' (with all those similar to it) but that there is something odd in my saying that we can, in the same way, understand 'murder' and other moral terms? In other words, why should it be thought that, in order for 'murder' to be meaningful, there must be some morally neutral type of action which must first be identified and only then declared to be wrong, rather than that, as I have suggested, it is by understanding why these acts are wrong that we know that they are murders? The answer seems clear: the objector does not believe that there is any object for the understanding in morals. That is to say, he is begging the very question which we are investigating, because he is presuming the non-cognitivity of ethics.

It is worth recalling the early arguments of the *Republic* once more. Cephalus and Polymarchus attempted to define 'justice' in morally neutral terms, and Socrates was able to show that the proposed definitions were inadequate. This shows that both Socrates and his companions understood the meaning of 'justice', for the latter offered plausible characterisations – no one, for example, suggested that a just act was one performed with the left hand or which took place between ten and twelve in the morning – and Socrates was able to propose suitable objections to the definitions, the validity of which his companions were able to recognise. All these performances presuppose an understanding of what justice is, and this tends to make one think that there is something to be understood, that moral thought is a distinctive kind of thought: distinctive, but still thought.

11. *Similarity and Moral Types*

The question before us hinges on the notion of 'similarity', a notion whose importance ranges far beyond the field of moral judgement. Part of the genius of the poet as well as of the scientist is to discover hitherto unrecognised similarities; and, in a humbler vein, the ability to use everyday words is dependent upon the ability to identify different things as similar to one another. Thus, for example, when Hare says that 'all value-judgements are covertly universal in character, which is the same as to say that they refer to, and express acceptance of, a standard which has an application to other similar instances',[45] he is saying something which is true, but which is, in one respect, a truism, and, in another, potentially misleading.

The statement is a truism in the sense that any judgement, not just a value-judgement, is likewise universal, since to use a word is to appeal to a standard (a 'definition', a 'meaning-rule') which governs that use. The statement is potentially misleading in that it lends itself to the interpretation that the similarity of the instances is independent of the application of the standard. It is instructive to compare this interpretation with the similarity-recognition involved in the normal use of words. We say of a person that he has learned the meaning of a word – i. e., the 'rule' or 'standard' which governs its use – when he can correctly identify specimens of its denotation and, conversely, when he knows the meaning of the word, then he can use it correctly. One cannot have one without the other. Now, in the possible interpretation which I have given to Hare's statement, what is being said is that in the use of some words, those, namely, which are used in value-judgements, one could correctly identify the members of a class without reference to the appropriate standard, which amounts to saying that one could use a word correctly without knowing its meaning.

The best, and probably the only, answer to this is that given by Hare himself to the effect that, since evaluative expressions are used not only to denote things but also to commend (or condemn) them, it is possible for someone to grasp the former aspect of the meaning (i. e., the 'descriptive' meaning), and thus be able to identify specimens, without understanding the latter aspect (i. e., the element of commendation). Such a person, although he could denote the proper things, could not be said to be using the word correctly because he would not be using it to commend those things, and this because he did not understand the full meaning of the word.[46] Hare illustrates this by coining the word 'doog' which is to carry the 'descriptive meaning', or denotative potential, of 'good' but which is bereft of the latter's commendatory force.[47] A man is 'doog', therefore, if, and only if, he is good, but in applying the neutral adjective one is merely saying that he is a certain type of man, whereas the use of the moral term commends him for being that type.

This explanation has some plausibility, but it does not stand up to closer scrutiny. The first thing that arouses one's suspicions is the fact that we have no words even remotely like 'doog' in our language, so that when Hare wants to tell us some of the characteristics of a 'doog' man he does this by telling us some of the things that he calls 'good'; that is, by referring to his moral standards. He tells us that the kind of man that he has in mind is 'for example a man who feeds his children, does not beat his wife, etc.'[48] I think that it is obvious that no one could continue this list of 'doog' characteristics without tacitly referring to the conventional moral standards that serve as its *rationale*. There is no empirical similarity between feeding children and abstaining from wife-beating except that both have something to do with family relations, and this is no help to one who wants to fill in the *etcetera* since, presumably, some 'doog' men do not have families and since not all familial behaviour is 'doog'.

Suppose someone says: 'Brown is similar to Jones because Brown feeds his children and Jones does not beat his wife.' The only detectable similarity in the respective behaviour of Brown and Jones is that each satisfies one of the duties of a married man; without the standard, there would be no similarity. In a society whose moral code prescribed both children-feeding and wife-beating, Brown and Jones would be thought to be behaving in quite different fashions.

It is no reply to say that all wife-beating is similar regardless of whether it is commended or condemned, because that is beside the point. The point is that 'doog' was supposed to denote all and only those things which we call 'good' with this difference, that one could understand its meaning without reference to morality. This, we saw, is not the case because, for example, the question of whether wife-beating or the abstinence therefrom is to count as a 'doog' characteristic cannot be answered without the prior moral judgement that it is, or is not, a 'good' characteristic. Which is to say, there is no morally neutral type of man that we could, if we wished, designate as 'doog' because the classification has coherence only from the moral point of view. 'Doog' is either a meaningless token or it means precisely the same as 'good'. I shall now explore this problem a bit further in order to show why it is no contingent fact that our language contains no words like 'doog'.

The question, as I mentioned, turns on the notion of 'similarity'. It is obvious, first of all, that 'being similar' is not some sort of property that things have like 'being red' or 'being rectangular'. Nor is it a relation like 'being taller than', because, if I say that A is taller than B, you know what I mean, assuming that A and B are the sort of things that have height, but if I say that A is similar to B, you do not, without further information, understand me. Similarity is a triadic relation of the form: A is similar to B in respect C. Since similarity is normally looked for within some context of meaning (one would say simply 'pick similar things' only in a game or an intelligence test), it is generally not sufficient that things be similar in any respect but in some *relevant* respect. Things which are similar in the relevant respects are said to be similar from the appropriate point of view, or within the appropriate context of meaning.

Thus, to use 'similar' meaningfully, there must be at least a tacit reference to the point of view from which the judgement of similarity is being made. It could be plausibly argued, although I shall not argue it here, that any two things are similar in *some* respect; it is certainly true that any two things are dissimilar in some respect, namely, in that respect by virtue of which they are distinguishable. It may well be, as, for example, in assembly line products, that the only discernible difference between two things is that they take up different spatial positions, but this is not always an irrelevant consideration.

All the ink in the same bottle is, presumably, of identical chemical composition, which is not altered if some of that ink is spilt onto a piece of paper. However, from the point of view of tidiness, this spatial differentiation is critical. One can imagine the short shrift that a student, even a chemistry student, would get from his teacher if he explained that his work was not really untidy since there is no chemical difference between ink in the bottle and ink on the paper. Let us suppose that the student takes to heart the lesson that inkspots on paper are untidy but that the following week he presents a paper with a coffee stain and protests that is not untidy since coffee and ink are chemically different. He clearly has not grasped the meaning of 'untidy', and one can imagine his presenting an indefinite series of papers with assorted, chemically different, blotches, each time protesting that this case is different from its predecessors. His teacher will not have taught him the required standards of tidiness – and thereby equipped him to identify new cases of untidiness – until he has got him to understand *why* it is that an inkspot is similar to a coffee stain and, in this respect, dissimilar to ink in the bottle. The point of this example (for which I am indebted to Kovesi) is that, since aspects which are irrelevant from one point of view can become significant when the terms of reference are changed, one cannot specify what are to count as relevant respects for the purpose of calling things 'similar' unless one knows the appropriate context of meaning. What I want to show, it should be clear, is that the attempt to specify moral types in morally neutral terms is like the attempt to specify 'tidiness' in chemical ('tidiness-neutral') terms.

With the foregoing in mind, let us consider what is entailed in the belief that the similarity between actions which is the basis for judging like cases alike is recognisable independently of the moral standard by which they are being judged. To say things are similar is to say that there is some point of view from which this similarity can be detected and that, in order to detect *this* similarity, this particular point of view must be taken. This is so because, without the point of view, the question of relevance will not have been decided.

An instructive comparison is provided by the Bernini colonnade in St Peter's Square. If one takes up the proper point of view – namely, one of the two *foci* of the ellipse – what is from any other vantage point an undifferentiated conglomeration of columns sorts itself into neat, rank-and-file order so that only the front rank is visible. The example is doubly instructive because, since there are two *foci*, there are two points of view from which everything falls into line, but with this difference: different columns fall behind each front-rank pillar in the two instances, and this could make a perceptible difference, since, if, for example, a scaffolding were strategically placed so as to be invisible from one point of view it would be visible from the other. The moral of this is that one can classify things the same way from only one point of view and that, although it is true that the same unclassified subject-matter can be classified from different points of view, the respective classifications will gather together different combinations of elements.

We can transfer this from the field of visual perception to a case of simple conceptual classification by imagining that someone has a collection of bits of plastic of assorted colours and shapes which he wants to sort out so that all the bits in a given pile will be similar. He can do this once from the point of view of colour and then from the point of view of shape and, in each instance, he will have exhaustively classified his collection, but the two sets of piles will not have been composed of the same mixtures of bits of plastic.

To move closer to the appropriate subject, let me recall that things which are similar from the point of view of chemistry are not so when one is thinking of tidiness.

In each of these instances the two opposed classifications are made from distinctive points of view and are themselves distinctive, which means that they are irreducibly different. One could not, for example, define shapes in terms of colours; nor could one give a list of chemical formulae, with accompanying spatio-temporal reference co-ordinates, which would help us notice the similarity between inkspots, coffee stains, unmade beds, etc. Even if every recorded case of untidiness were to be given its proper formula, there are some of us who are capable of finding new and creative ways to be untidy! Taking up the point of view of colour or shape, or of chemistry or tidiness, is thus similar to taking up a position at one of the *foci* of the ellipse in our visual example.

What is being said, then, when it is asserted that cases which are alike for the purpose of moral judgement are similar from some other, morally neutral, point of view? I think that it is clear that what is being asserted is that there is no distinctive 'moral point of view', and it is not difficult to see why such an assertion is made by both sides in the debate about naturalism. The naturalist obviously needs to deny that there is a distinctive moral point of view because, as we saw, there is no logical transition between concepts formed from different points of view. The anti-naturalist position equally requires this denial because, if there were such a point of view, it would mean that there was a distinctive way of understanding and interpreting human action, which we call the 'moral' way, and moral activity (the making of moral judgements, the engaging in moral inquiry, etc.) would be, therefore, a pre-eminently 'cognitive' or 'rational' mode of behaviour, with all that this implies. One could not sensibly say, that is, that the acceptance of moral standards was to take up an attitude or to adopt a policy about certain kinds of things except in the innocuous, and cognitivist, sense that the attitudes or decisions follow upon the recognition that these things are right or wrong, because, if there is a distinctive moral point of view, different actions are of the same *kind* only because they are being judged to be right or wrong by the same standard.

I want to show now that there *is* a moral point of view, that we have a distinctive way of classifying actions with regard to their being right or wrong, and that these classifications cannot be specified in morally neutral terms. I shall go about this by first showing that 'murder' is such a classification, and then by showing that the same argument applies to all those types of action which involve the infringement of the 'rights' or 'interests' or 'inclinations' of others; that is, those types which used to be treated under the heading of 'justice'. If I am successful in this, I shall have made my point because I shall have demonstrated that there is a vast tract (some writers would say it was the whole) of the moral territory in which the questions which arise cannot be settled in terms of facts and logic alone, which is what both the naturalists and the anti-naturalists have been trying to do, as Prior has rightly pointed out.[49]

12. *'Murder' as a Moral Type*

To begin with, we can locate 'murder' on the conceptual map as a special type of 'deliberate homicide'. (I shall not be concerned with the aspect designated by 'deliberate'. This is not because I do not think that it is of the utmost importance; indeed, I think that the question of personal responsibility is one crying out for adequate treatment. However, it is not the question which I am trying to answer here.)

One can distinguish different types of homicide from various points of view. For example, from the point of view of method, we can divide homicides into 'shootings', 'poisonings', 'stabbings', etc. From the point of view of the identity of the victim, we can distinguish 'regicide', 'fratricide', 'infanticide', etc. It is clear, I think, that we will not find 'murder' in either of these divisions.

What is the point of view from which homicides are divided so that one of the divisions is 'murder'? Earlier I gave a few examples of 'murder': killing a person in order to inherit his money, or to marry his wife, or because he is a Jew. That is, it has something to do with the slayer's reason for killing his victim. It is not, of course, that there is anything that one could notice about these reasons taken in themselves. For one thing, there is no empirical similarity between, for example, a person's possessing money that one wants to inherit and a person's being a Jew. Also, there are quite unexceptionable things that one could do for these same reasons; for example, one could advise someone to make a will in order to inherit his money, if that is what he wants to do with his money, and one could serve someone kosher food because he is a Jew. What is relevant to the classification of an act as 'murder' is not the reason *in itself*, but as a *reason-for-killing*; not *what* the reason is, but *that* it is not a good reason for killing someone. Underlying the concept of 'murder' is the belief that the taking of human life requires a special justification. Murders are homicides which lack that justification; 'murder' means 'unjustifiable homicide'.

Thus, when we want to judge like cases alike, we are not looking for some morally neutral similarity between them, but for a similarity in accordance with certain standards of justification. To take a famous instance of judging like cases alike, King David could have correctly pointed out to the Prophet Nathan that there were several quite obvious empirical differences between killing a man in order to steal his ewe lamb and killing a man in order to marry his wife; for example, a ewe lamb is much less valuable than a wife and, also, one can quite easily steal a man's lamb without killing him, but it is not so easy to marry a man's wife without somehow disposing of him. The two cases, David might have said, are not at all similar. He did not say this, of course, and he would have been mistaken if he had because the cases are alike; the empirical differences between them are irrelevant. But they are alike only in this, that both in the fable and in the real-life story the reasons for killing a man were not good reasons; that is to say, they are alike only from the moral point of view.

Murders are alike, and are distinguished from other homicides, in accordance with the standards which determine which reasons can justify the taking of human life. Take away those standards and the class of murders would disappear without trace into the general class of homicides; which is another way of saying that there is no morally neutral type of action about which one could adopt the policy, or draw the conclusion, that it is wrong. If there is no such neutral type, there could be no neutral description which would denote all and only murders.

It might be supposed that, even if there is no single neutral description which would correctly express the sense of 'murder', this might be accomplished by a disjunction of descriptions. However, this is fallacious on two counts: (a) Let us say that we have compiled a list of n descriptive expressions such that the applicability of one of these expressions to an action is a sufficient condition for calling that action a murder. This disjunction would not adequately express the meaning of 'murder' because to show that the applicability of one of these descriptions is a sufficient condition for the applicability of 'murder' is not to show that it is a necessary condition. If there are $n + 1$, or more, kinds of murder, we should not be able to recognise these new kinds by relying on the old list; yet it is a normal characteristic of our grasping the meaning of a word (Searle calls this the 'projective' quality of meaning) [50] that it enables us to recognise new and unusual instances. (b) It is difficult to make sense of the suggestion that the meaning of a word be tied to a disjunction of descriptive expressions, for if these are logically independent expressions (and otherwise there would be no reason to disjoin them), there is no apparent reason why the things they designate should be thought of as one kind of thing. 'Murder' would thus have as many meanings as there were situations to which it applied; i.e., it would be meaningless. The case is, of course, that the concept of murder is the principle which unifies logically independent descriptions such as 'shooting someone in order to marry his wife' and 'poisoning someone in order to inherit his money'. It is by relying upon one's standards that one knows what sort of neutral descriptions to look for. 'Murder' is thus like 'untidy', 'unsafe' and 'table'. This topic will be further developed in Part Two (section 24).

13.   *Standards of Justification*

The standard which determines what reasons will justify the taking of a life is similar, in some obvious respects, to a standard of argument which determines what reasons will justify the making of an assertion. This is a valuable comparison because logical notions (which perform a similar function in relation to discourse as ethical notions perform towards behaviour) are also such that they cannot be translated into neutral terms.

Let us consider, for example, the notion of a 'bad argument'. Would it be possible to devise a description which would be devoid of logical assessment and yet would denote all and only bad arguments? One reason to make one think that this could not be done is that the use of words like 'true' and 'false' – which one might naturally want to employ – would be precluded because it is perfectly clear that these normative terms cannot be given a neutral description. If it is not immediately clear, one need only refer to A. Tarski's demonstration that 'true' cannot be defined in the same language as the statements to which it is applied.[51] Another reason is that most of the arguments which we come across in daily life cannot be cast into any strict, rule-governed, form. There are almost always reasons for, and reasons against, accepting a conclusion, which means that one cannot avoid the need to make logical assessments.

It might be supposed that there is a counter-example in the first-order predicate calculus, which has been shown to be complete and consistent, and which is, therefore, completely rule-governed. In other words, the validity of inferences within the calculus is strictly decided by the mechanical application of the rules in such a way that, if an argument violates rule R, this is sufficient to call it an invalid, or 'bad', argument. However, this is a mistake. In the first place, the most it would show is that some types of bad argument can be neutrally described, and considering how little can be said within the first-order predicate calculus this is a severe limitation. Secondly, the calculus does not provide rules for deciding such crucial questions as whether or not the terms are being used univocally. Finally, it is not the case that 'inference I is invalid' means 'I violates R'. The role of R as a criterion is not independent of the notion of logical validity, because this notion is the standard according to which R, S, ... etc., are acknowledged as rules of inference and which thus provides the warrant for their use as criteria. I is invalid because it violates R if, and only if, one accepts R as a criterion of validity (otherwise one could apply a well-known type of argument to show that all that was being said was that I violates R because I violates R, and this would say nothing about its being a good or bad argument), but this can be done only by relying on logical standards. We encounter, once more, the confusion between meaning and criteria.

Thus, moral concepts are structurally similar to logical concepts in that both types contain, as an essential element of their meaning, an irreducible standard for the assessment of justifying reasons – in the one case for the performance of actions, in the other for the making of assertions. This should not be surprising since ethics and logic are both normative disciplines, and it shows that there is no more reason to deny that ethical thought is rational, or that it is a way of understanding and interpreting experience within its own sphere, than there is reason to deny these things of logic.

It is possible for a philosopher to take a hard line here and deny that either of these normative disciplines is cognitive. Such a proposal is, of course, self-defeating, since it makes it impossible for anyone who defends it to offer any reasons why his arguments ought to be accepted, but we can certainly allow that someone can hold this opinion if he wants to. However, if he wants to say that logic (along with science and common sense) is non-cognitive, we surely can demand that he stop treating ethics as if it were in some way specially deficient in this respect. If even the 'relations between ideas' is to be removed as a subject of rational inquiry, then we are left with very little else to go on.

It might be objected that I have restated the question instead of answering it, that all I have shown is that what needs specification is not a type of action but a type of reason for acting. 'To adopt the policy that murder is wrong' is translated to mean: 'To adopt the policy that certain kinds of reason will justify killing a man and that certain other kinds will not'; but this puts us back at the beginning.

In answer to this, one might note first of all that the idea of specifying types of justifying reasons lacks the *prima facie* plausibility of specifying types of action. We all know what it means to specify a type of action; for example, 'No smoking!' specifies, and forbids, a type of action. But it is not at all clear how one would go about specifying types of justifying reasons. What reasons one will accept as justifying the taking of a human life depends upon the value that one puts on human life, and it is difficult to see how this can be stated in value-free terms, which is what is required if the value of the reasons is to be made consequent upon the decision to adopt a policy about them. Is one to suppose that a complete definition of 'murder' would be a list of all the possible reasons that anyone could have for killing a man with each reason marked with its value as a justification for killing, rather like an international exchange list of currencies? This would be like trying to define 'tidiness' in chemical terms or like offering a directory of names as a definition of 'man'. The whole point of a concept is that it enables one to recognise new specimens, that it defines an *open*, not a closed, set.

Moreover, even when one can come up with a reasonably good example of a justifying reason, one has not eliminated the element of assessment. For example, most people think that a person is justified in taking another's life if the other is assaulting him with a deadly weapon with the intent to kill. However, they would not think so if the aggressor were a child with a kitchen knife and the defendant a trained policeman or soldier, nor would they think that a convicted murderer has the right to kill the executioner. Even 'self-defence' must be qualified with words like 'necessary' and 'legitimate'; i. e., with built-in norms. One cannot 'factor out' the element of assessment.

Not the least ludicrous aspect of the notion that the concept of murder is something like an exchange list of justifying reasons is the fact that no one does, or could, carry such a list around with him but that people do use the word 'murder' sensibly. Even if this lack of specification were only a contingent fact, which it is not, it is, nevertheless, decisive evidence against the belief that the standard in accordance with which murders are condemned is a policy which people have decided to adopt. We all know, and if we forget Chomsky and Polanyi are always there to remind us, that our use of words is governed by many rules which we could not explicitly state. The standard which determines what reasons justify killing a man is one such rule for the use of the word 'murder'.

Even if it could be stated, the fact is that people follow this rule who are not able to state it. There is much about this ability to follow unknown rules which requires explanation, but one thing we can say for sure is that it is not the result of a decision. One cannot make a decision about something that one knows nothing about. The contrast is clear between this sort of rule and the sort that can be the result of a deliberate choice; for example, a stipulated definition. It is a necessary feature of a stipulated definition that it can be stipulated; one cannot stipulate the unspecifiable. The attempt to interpret moral standards on the model of axiom-choice or of stipulated definitions breaks down when one is confronted with the notion of choosing unstatable axioms or of stipulating undefinable definitions.

14. *Some Corollaries*

The realisation that the moral standard implicit in the concept of murder is the standard which determines what reasons are to be admitted as a justification for the taking of human life helps to explain some facts which might otherwise seem rather mysterious. It also, as I shall show, sheds a whole new light on the nature of moral inquiry. The perplexing questions that this knowledge helps to answer are: How is it that two people who both agree that murder is wrong can have different moral standards in this respect (or, what amounts to the same thing: How is it that moral standards can change without changing the words which express them)? And: If 'murder is wrong' is analytic, how is it that a person who disagreed with the moral standard expressed in that statement could still use 'murder' meaningfully?

To go about answering the first question, we must get clear about what is involved in saying that two people have different standards. Do they have different concepts of, or mean something different by, 'murder'? In a sense they do, and in another sense they do not. They do not have different 'formal' concepts because they agree that 'murder' means 'unjustifiable homicide'. This provides the frame for any possible discussion of their standards; it sets the terms of reference for the discussion, the limits beyond which the discussion cannot go. For example, neither of them will call a case 'murder' in which nobody has been killed. If you will, it ensures that they are playing the same game even if, as it happens, they are following different rules. However, they do differ in their 'material' or 'real' concepts; that is, they have different concepts if we take 'concept' in the sense defined by Gilbert Ryle as 'the functioning of a word', or by P. T. Geach in the following: 'It will be a *sufficient* condition for James's having the concept of a *so-and-so* that he should have mastered the intelligent use (including the use in made-up sentences) of a word for *so-and-so* in some language.' (His italics.) [52] Along these same lines, I would say that a concept, in this sense, is the *rationale* behind the use, or which controls the use, of a word.

What happens, then, when two people agree that murder is wrong but have different standards in this respect is that they fill in the same formal frame with different content because each is selecting his elements in accordance with a different *rationale*. Since the formal frame determines the range of the concept, provides the context of inquiry, it is itself an important, and controlling, feature of the *rationale* which guides the use of the word. Therefore, we can expect to find aid in answering the question of how people develop different standards by considering how they might go about supplying a content to their formal concepts. I have mentioned before, and shall have occasion to mention again, that it is always important to ask concerning a moral problem: Why is there thought to be a problem here? In this instance, the question is: Why do you think that homicide requires a special justification? The answers that one gets to this question will be the first statement of the *rationale* that controls the person's use of 'murder'. I shall pursue this line of inquiry in the following chapters; for now, I think that it is clear that radically different answers to this question will lead to different rules of selection, that is, to different moral standards.

One important fact that emerges from the foregoing is that, not only does 'murder' classify its elements from a distinctive, moral point of view, but also that the moral standard is not an isolated piece of conceptual equipment; it is intimately bound up with, and under the control of, a great many other beliefs that the agent holds, notably about human life. An illuminating comparison can be made with the concept of 'sacrilege'. People of quite different religious beliefs will all agree that 'sacrilege' is wrong; i. e., they have the same formal concept. However, it is clear that what, say, a Protestant and a Catholic, or, even more so, a Christian and a Hindu, will condemn as a sacrilege varies considerably; they have different moral standards in this respect. It is also clear that the source of this difference is the difference in their respective beliefs about what is sacred.

With the help of the notion of sacrilege, we can now answer the other question, how it is that a man who did not think that murder was wrong could still use 'murder' intelligently. This is like asking how a completely secularised man could use 'sacrilege' intelligibly. He is using it in the 'inverted comma' sense: 'what others call "sacrilege" '; or, to be more precise, he would have to specify that the 'others' were Christians or Hindus or whatever. That is, he would be able to recognise instances of 'sacrilege' only by relying on the moral standards of others. There is nothing that *he* would call a sacrilege; for example, he would never condemn an act as a sacrilege – as the destruction of property, perhaps, or as an insult to religious people but never *qua* sacrilege. For the man to whom nothing is sacred, nothing is a sacrilege.

The same is true of the moral deviant who does not think that murder is wrong. The fact is that he does not believe that there is such a thing as 'murder' (i. e., unjustifiable homicide) and, if he uses that word, he is denoting what certain specified 'others' mean by 'murder'. As was the case with the secularised man, the moral sceptic's lack of a moral standard in this regard is bound up with certain other of his beliefs about the world. What he is saying is that homicide does not require a special justification, that shooting a man is like shooting a grouse or like picking a rose, and it is not difficult to see what far-ranging implications this belief would have in his conceptual scheme.

There are some further conclusions which follow from this analysis of 'murder'. It is clear, for one thing, that 'murder is wrong' is not the expression of a moral standard, in the sense that one could not rely upon this statement as a guide to the making of moral judgements. It is the mere statement of the truism that unjustifiable homicide is unjustified. Therefore, the person who says, 'This act is wrong because it is murder', is not guilty of concealing the premiss that murder is wrong which he must justify or, failing that, prescribe, because his reasoning is logically complete: to say that something is murder is to say that it is wrong. I am not saying that the moral judgement is not a 'substantial', as opposed to a 'logical' or 'merely verbal', judgement; what I am saying is that the substance comes from the judgement, 'This is murder', not from the judgement, 'Murder is wrong'. I shall demonstrate later that moral judgements are not unique in this respect; that is, that, generally, statements like 'This is a man', 'This is a tree', 'This is a table', 'He is tall', are 'substantial' judgements. Nor am I saying that people do not have moral standards about homicide, but only 'descriptive' standards about the use of 'murder'. 'Murder' expresses a moral concept; to call something a murder is to make a moral judgement.

15. *Other Moral Concepts*

In order to judge like cases alike, one must be able to tell which cases are alike, which is the function of one's moral concepts. The critical question about these concepts, we saw, is whether the acts which they classify constitute distinctive moral types or whether they are similar to each other anyway, regardless of what moral positions we take about them. Is there a 'moral point of view', that is to say, a distinctive way of understanding and interpreting human action which is irreducible to concepts formed from any other vantage point? Although they draw different conclusions from the belief, both sides in the controversy about naturalism have said, in effect, that there is no such point of view. Like cases are alike independently of our moral beliefs; even people with different standards could recognise this similarity. I have shown that, in at least one instance, this contention is false. 'Murder' classifies actions from a distinctive, moral point of view; that is, this concept enables us to see a similarity between cases which could not be otherwise detected. People with different moral standards would see different acts as similar and dissimilar. Moreover, the consideration of 'murder' has given us some idea of what the moral point of view is like: it has to do with the judgement that the performance of certain types of action (in this instance, the taking of human life) requires a special justifying reason. We also saw, that, in the case of 'murder' and, by the way, of 'sacrilege', the moral point of view, although distinctive, has intimate links with a great many of the agent's other beliefs about the world, that moral standards are under the rational control of those beliefs. These considerations have an obvious relevance to, and open up certain possibilities concerning, the nature of moral inquiry which I shall take up in Part Two.

To the present point, I think that I have established my case by showing that there is, in at least one instance, a distinctive moral point of view. I have, that is to say, provided a counter-example to the theories of the naturalists and of the anti-naturalists. There is one range of moral activity, and that an extremely important one, in which one cannot derive moral judgements from factual considerations and in which one cannot sensibly be said to be engaging in some non-cognitive activity, such as taking up attitudes or adopting policies. Nor is it difficult to see how one could extend this range. One thinks immediately of 'stealing' and 'lying'; they clearly are capable of the same treatment as 'murder' if one substitutes for 'taking a human life' something like 'taking human property' and 'telling falsehoods', respectively. Since lying is rather the more difficult of the two, I shall show how the analysis applies to it.

The chief difficulty about lying is that 'lie' has not been clearly distinguished, either in common or in philosophic usage, from 'telling a falsehood'. For example, Aquinas defined 'lie' as '*locutio contra mentem*' and helped set off the long train of casuistry about 'dissimulation' and 'mental reservation' for which Cardinal Newman was called to task by Charles Kingsley in the last century. In the same vein, writers who want to be paradoxical sometimes conflate the notions of 'murder' and 'homicide' and then make the startling statement that murder is sometimes justified.[53] What they mean, of course, is not that unjustifiable homicide is sometimes justified, but that homicide is sometimes justified, or, perhaps, that what some people call 'murder' is not really murder. The conflation of 'lie' and 'falsehood' has not, of course, always had this paradoxical purpose. Writers, like Kant, who were looking for a type of moral activity that they could get their rational 'teeth' into thought that they had found what they wanted in the lie. It is not hard to demonstrate that all communication between human beings would break down if people did not generally obey the moral rule that telling falsehoods is wrong, just as it would break down if they did not obey the language rules which govern our use of words. Although not all writers have come to Kant's rigorous conclusions, the general tendency has been to treat 'lie' as meaning 'telling a falsehood', and this has led to some well-known anomalies.

As before, I am not attempting to dictate usage. I can, if you will, say as I did with murder, that I am talking about 'lie$_1$', which means 'unjustifiable lie'. It does not matter that some people, such as Kant, think that 'lie$_1$' is equivalent to 'speaking a falsehood', because the reasons for saying this are something that we can discuss. After all, some pacifists set such high standards of justification that all homicides are murders, and some philosophers set such high standards of argumentation, especially when it comes to justifying moral judgements, that nothing short of a strict, deductive proof will suffice, which is to say, that no justification is possible. It is not my purpose to argue for or against any particular moral standard about lying, but to say something about how the concept 'lie' functions in the making of moral judgements.

We are concerned with how people judge cases alike and how they distinguish right from wrong when it comes to deceiving others. By common standards, people think that it is all right to say what they know to be untrue if this is done, for example, in order to make a joke, or to test students, or to take a role in a play, or to save someone's life, but that it is wrong if it is done in order to steal someone's money, or to avoid responsibilities, or to enlist people's aid in some project which they would shun if they knew the truth. We judge cases to be alike, not because of any similarities in the content of the communications or in the skill or technique of the deception, but from the point of view of the reason-for-deceiving; that is, with a view to whether or not it is a good reason for saying what is known to be false.

'Lie', when it is used as a moral concept to judge like cases alike, functions like 'murder' in that it brings out similarities which are discernible only from the moral point of view. The two concepts differ, of course, in subject-matter, and this makes a big difference in what counts as a justifying reason. For example, a man who thinks that it is all right to deceive somebody for a joke probably does not think that it is all right to kill somebody for a joke because of his belief that deception is not so important, nor so irrevocable, as killing. But the point is that it *is* what he believes about deception, or, more precisely, why he thinks that deception requires a special justification, that determines what his moral standard is ˙in this regard.

Since there are other ways we can harm people besides killing or deceiving them, there are other moral concepts which deal with these interests from the moral point of view. It is not that *any* interest of others generates this requirement for a special justification; e. g., I do not think that I need a special reason for drawing the curtains at night because it goes against my curious neighbour's interest in what is happening in my house. One must judge the importance and legitimacy of interests; and one must be able to arbitrate between conflicts of interest. It is clear, I think, that these judgements of importance, like the standards for 'murder' and 'lie', are not made in isolation, but against the background and under the control of the agent's set of relevant beliefs. Further, one could devise arguments, similar to that which I have devised about 'murder', to show that there are some acts, like promise-keeping, the failure to do which requires special justification. From the moral point of view one can detect positive obligations as well as negative prohibitions. However, my purpose has been to show that there *is* a moral point of view, not to enumerate the objects which can be seen from there.

There is a set of apparent counter-examples to my argument, although one suspects that those who would be inclined to disagree with my position would not be inclined to set much store by them either. I refer to the rules that people make in what are sometimes misleadingly called matters of 'temperance'; rules, for example, about the use of alcohol, narcotics or sex. These rules clearly do specify types of action which are identifiable apart from one's moral opinion about them, and people who disagree about their morality are unquestionably talking about the same things. I shall say a little, but only a very little, about these matters.

For one thing, the fact that these rules do not fit into my description of the moral point of view, if it is a fact, proves only that they need a different explanation; it does not prove that I was mistaken in my identification of a moral point of view. It might prove, and I tend to think that this is true of some such rules, that they do not deserve to be called 'moral', that they represent some less developed way of dealing with human conduct, like the rules that parents make for children. Secondly, in as much as these matters are condemned because of the harm which is being done to others – as, for example, heavy drinking can be condemned because it impairs a man's ability to support his family or adultery because it is offensive to the betrayed spouse – they clearly are capable of the same treatment as murder and lying. Finally, if we approach these matters with the question, 'Why is there thought to be a moral problem?', we can uncover what we have come to recognise as the moral point of view: one gets the statement of an underlying *rationale* and the element of assessment, with the consequent flexibility, which is a common feature of moral standards. An excellent example is provided by Paul Ramsey, when he argues that the decision of what is to count as 'premarital sex' cannot be determined by reference to the participation of the relevant persons in a formal ceremony, but must be judged in the light of their mutual commitments. [54]

16. *Similarity and Validity*

To say that *A* is similar to *B* in respect of *C* is to say that something is the case regardless of one's personal choices or attitudes. A judgement of similarity is a judgement which claims independent validity and which is, in this respect, of the same order as a report of perception, a scientific conclusion or an historical judgement. In other words, to say that *A* is similar to *B* in respect of *C* implies the belief that anyone who would consider *A* and *B* from the appropriate point of view – that in which *C* is considered to be a relevant respect – would detect, and acknowledge, this similarity. Since moral judgements are based on the recognition of similarity, they make, to that extent, similar interpersonal claims. If it can be shown further, that the making of a moral judgement presupposes the validity of the standard which is employed – which standard determines what is to count as a relevant respect – then it would follow that moral judgements claim interpersonal validity.

Let us recall Popper's notion of 'background knowledge' which we encountered in Lakatos's criticism of the principle of falsifiability (section 5 above). Popper defines this as 'all those things which we accept (tentatively) as unproblematic while we are testing the theory'.[55] It seems reasonably evident that there must be some background knowledge of this nature in any inquiry, that there must be some terms of reference which are not themselves in question but which are being relied upon in order to question something else. It is not that these terms are thought to be unquestionable, but that they are not, during this inquiry, being called in question. If they are to be criticised, this would be a different inquiry and would require that there be other terms of reference which would be uncritically accepted as background knowledge. Polanyi illustrates this point vividly and persuasively:

> . . . Suppose a paper is published under the title: *An Explanation of 'Extra-Sensory Perception'*, and another in reply to it entitled: *An 'Explanation' of Extra-Sensory Perception*. Guided by the quotation marks we recognise immediately that the first paper regards extra-sensory perception as spurious, while the second accredits it as genuine and discredits, on the contrary, the explanation suggested for it in the first paper.
>
> Descriptive words written down as part of a sentence without quotation marks around them are confidently relied upon: they accredit the substantial character of the conception which they convey and its appositeness to the matter in hand. I shall call this the *confident* or *direct* use of a word. By contrast, a descriptive word used in quotation

marks . . . is used in a *sceptical* or *oblique* fashion. Such use calls into question either the reality of the conception evoked by the word, or its applicability to the case in point. . . .

By contrasting the oblique use of words with their direct use, we can now show formally that these risks of confident utterances are unavoidable. We may place a word in quotation marks, while using language confidently through the rest of a sentence. But the questioning of *each* word *in turn* would never question *all at the same time*. Accordingly, it would never reveal a comprehensive error which underlies our entire descriptive idiom. We can of course write down a text and withdraw our confidence from all its words simultaneously, by putting each descriptive word between quotation marks. But then none of the words would mean anything and the whole text would be meaningless. The hazards of confidence inherent in the act of attaching a meaning at least to some set of descriptive terms are ineradicable.[56]

There is one aspect of the Popperian notion of 'background knowledge' which requires closer examination. Popper admits that we must hold some knowledge uncritically, but says that we do this 'tentatively'. What is the sense of 'tentatively' as used here? It is clearly meant to soften, to add an air of intellectual respectability to, the practice of accepting beliefs uncritically, but is it a legitimate use of the word? Let us consider how the word is used in other contexts. If we say, for example, that a skater is proceeding tentatively, we mean that he is staying close to the shore, that he is holding the hand of a well-grounded companion or grasping a tree trunk, that he carefully puts a foot forward making sure that he does not entrust it with all his weight until he is assured that the ice will not give in, etc. We should certainly not say of a skater who is dashing about the lake, executing intricate manoeuvres, that he is relying upon the ice 'tentatively'. But the latter seems to be an exact parallel with the acceptance of a belief as unproblematic and relying upon it as a critical tool.

Perhaps 'tentatively' as used to refer to background knowledge means 'accepted as true although it has not been conclusively proven to be certainly true', but this would be such a stretching of the meaning of the word as to amount to a distortion. Our confident skater, especially if he has had a philosophical training, would surely admit the possibility that the ice might crack at any moment, but this would not entitle us to say that his reliance upon the ice was 'tentative'. Nor could the acceptance of background knowledge be passed off simply as a methodological decision. If the truth or falsity of the subject of inquiry is at stake, this could never be settled by the mere decision to accept some belief as background knowledge, since this would be to say, not that the conclusion is true, but that one has decided that it is true, and this is not quite the same thing. Furthermore, one would never make a methodological decision to accept as true a proposition which one knew to be riddled with inner contradictions, or even a proposition which one seriously suspected to be false, except, perhaps, in order to effect a *reductio ad absurdum*.

Thus, the reliance upon unproblematic background knowledge as a critical standard in the appraisal of the truth of some other belief is the acceptance of the background knowledge as true, even though one would be willing to admit that it is not unquestionably true. To call this acceptance 'tentative' is to give that word an unusual meaning, quite different from that which it normally has, for to rely upon a belief uncritically is to display the greatest confidence in its truth for all that one admits the theoretical possibility of its being false. Furthermore, if this belief were to be subjected to criticism, there would be something else equally questionable which was being held as unproblematic background knowledge. The only way to avoid this would be to have a sufficient store of absolutely, and unquestionably, true beliefs to serve, whenever required, as background knowledge. This is a serious problem in the theory of knowledge,[57] but we need not follow it up here. What is relevant to our present point is that it be clear that to rely confidently upon a belief as unproblematic background knowledge is to presume the truth of that belief.

In any piece of ethical inquiry, as in scientific inquiry, there are beliefs which are held as unproblematic within that inquiry. Let us consider, for example, two people who are disputing the morality of capital punishment, and let us suppose that the particular point they are trying to settle is whether or not capital punishment is a deterrent to crime. Since factual accuracy about irrelevant facts is irrelevant, this dispute presumes that the deterrent-value of capital punishment is relevant to its morality. A person who believed that the State never, under any circumstances, had the right to take a human life – or, on the other side, a person who thought that capital punishment was justified on purely retributive grounds ('Let them get what's coming to them.') – would not think that statistical evidence that capital punishment is a deterrent to crime meant anything one way or the other so far as its morality is concerned. Since the relevance of facts to a moral judgement is determined by the appropriate moral standard, to presume the relevance of certain facts is to presume the appropriateness of the standard which determines that relevance; in this case, it is to presume that the deterrence of crime is a sufficient reason to justify the killing of certain criminals.

A standard which is the appropriate standard for the assessment of a given type of behaviour is what we call a 'valid' standard. Our conclusion is that to engage in an ethical inquiry in which the relevance of certain facts is accepted is to presume the validity of the moral standard which is being employed. If a person denies the validity of the standard, he cannot, as we saw, consistently engage in the inquiry since he would see it as the discussion of irrelevancies. If a person doubts the validity of the norm, his participation in the inquiry would be of a hypothetical nature; 'If you accept this norm, then proof of its deterrent-value would justify capital punishment, so let us study this question with the understanding that I am not yet sure about the validity of the standard.' Even if such a man were to accept the factual evidence as conclusive, he would not thereby be committed to a moral judgement about capital punishment because the hypothetical condition has not been satisfied. The man has not, that is to say, been engaged in an ethical inquiry at all, but in a statistical inquiry about the deterrent-value of capital punishment. He would be engaged in ethical inquiry if he were to examine the validity of the doubtful standard, but he would be relying during this inquiry upon other norms whose validity he did not question.

The judgement that A is similar to B in respect C claims interpersonal validity, as we saw. If C is a respect which is relevant for saying that things are similar from the moral point of view, the judgement that A is similar to B is a moral judgement which claims interpersonal validity. We have seen that a moral judgement is of the form, 'action a is right (or wrong) because it is of moral type T', and this is to say that a is similar to other t's in the relevant respects. If the moral standard which determines which respects are relevant is a valid standard, the moral judgement that a is T claims interpersonal validity. Since the very inquiry whether, and a $fortiori$ the judgement that, a is right or wrong presumes the validity of the relevant moral standard, moral judgements claim interpersonal validity.

To say that moral judgements make a claim to interpersonal validity is not to assert that moral judgements claim infallibility any more than the claim that a scientific explanation is correct in an assertion of infallibility. What is being asserted when we make a moral judgement is the $claim$, which may or may not be justified, that anyone who considers the case properly ought to agree that what we think to be right is right.

17. *Further Arguments for the Interpersonal Claim*

We have seen that, because they are based on the recognition of similarity, moral judgements claim interpersonal validity. The conclusion that moral judgements make such a claim can be supported by two other arguments: one based on the structure of the moral judgement, the other on the fact of universalisation.

The first argument is that a moral judgement makes a universal claim upon the judgements of others because, in the making of such a judgement, one believes that one is applying a valid standard correctly, which is incompatible with the belief that others might be justified in disagreeing; for if a person did not believe that others ought to agree with his judgement, it would mean that he thought that there was sufficient reason to doubt either the validity of the norm or the correctness of the application, or both. In any case, he would consider unwarranted the judgement that the course of action in question was right, when *ex hypothesi* he considers it warranted.

This argument holds regardless of the degree of conviction with which the judgement is made. If one is not sure whether something is right or wrong, then one thinks that others should also be unsure, and one would, for example, think that another person who was definite about such a case was mistaken. It is certainly true that we frequently must make decisions in questionable cases. When we do, we say something like: 'This is a most difficult situation, but for such-and-such reasons I think that this is the right course of action.' We admit, that is, that there are good reasons for holding a contrary opinion, but deny that these are strong enough to override the reasons which support the judgement; which is to say, we think that the contrary opinion is mistaken.

'But what', it might be asked, 'of a situation which is so perplexing that neither set of reasons is more authoritative than the other? One must decide, but one surely cannot claim that others ought to agree with this decision.' But how does one decide, if every possible avenue has been explored – every known principle has been examined, every similar case, including those in which one's role is reversed, has been considered, every foreseeable consequence has been weighed, etc. – and still the metaphorical scales remain balanced? It is no good to say; 'Make up your mind and live with it!' because one is obviously trying to decide what one will have to live with and can find no reason for choosing one or the other of the possibilities. In such a case, one can only employ some device of random selection (e.g. flipping a coin) and trust to one's luck that things do not turn out too badly, and it is true that one could hardly claim that others ought to agree that the course of action decided upon was right.

However, this is not a counter-example to my argument. A person who makes a random choice of a course of action is not logically committed to a universal prescription of that course of action in similar situations, since it was not his judgement that this was the right course of action. His universalised moral judgement is not: 'In cases like this one ought to do so-and-so'; but: 'Cases like this are insoluble, therefore one has to choose a course of action at random.' The latter judgement *does* make a claim to interpersonal validity.

It is worth noting that those theories which deny that moral judgements claim interpersonal validity are saying in effect, that all moral judgements are of the coin-flipping variety (otherwise, they would have to admit that some reasons are more authoritative than others, which contradicts their basic tenet). This implies that no choice of a course of action, since all such choices are random choices, commits one to a universal prescription of that course of action in similar situations. One cannot consistently hold that moral judgements are universalisable and that they are not justifiable.

It might be objected that my first argument in favour of saying that moral judgements make a universal claim on the judgements of others proves only that they claim validity for those who accept the same standards. It is true, the objection would go, that we justify our moral judgements by references to our moral standards, but since others subscribe to different standards, we cannot claim that they ought to agree with our judgements; from different premises, one draws different conclusions.

There are several senses in which this objection may be taken. In the first sense the objection states that one cannot *expect* that people with different standards will agree with one's judgements. The answer to this, obviously, is that I did not say that one believes that everyone *will* agree with one's moral judgements, but that they *ought* to. Since the making of a claim does not guarantee its satisfaction, moral judgements are not always, if ever, universally accepted. In his discussion of scientific discovery, Polanyi makes a useful distinction: 'I speak not of an *established* universality, but of a universal *intent*, for the scientist cannot know whether his claims will be accepted. They may prove false, or, though true, may fail to carry conviction. He may even expect that his conclusions will prove unacceptable, and in any case their acceptance will not guarantee him their truth. To claim validity for a statement merely declares that it *ought* to be accepted by all.' (His italics.)[58]

The important point, as I take it, that Polanyi is making is that the validity of the claim is independent of, and logically prior to, its acceptance. Thus, even if nobody agrees with one's judgement, while this is no doubt a good reason to re-examine, it is not a good reason for changing that judgement, because it rests on grounds other than the actual acceptance by others. This has obvious relevance to the question of ethical relativity: widespread divergence of belief in moral matters does not constitute a refutation of 'objective' theories of moral judgement, though it is a phenomenon which requires explanation from such theories. As the argument develops, we shall see that the intricate logical structure of the conceptual scheme employed in the making of moral judgements is enough, even apart from other important factors, to lead one to expect serious disagreements to arise and to permit one to claim that one is right without needing to accuse those who disagree of bad faith or stupidity.

In his article, 'The Objectivity of History', Passmore considers the criterion: 'In objective inquiries, conclusions are reached which are universally acceptable.'[59] His conclusion is that 'if we are satisfied with nothing less than . . . [what] all men the least rational will accept as final, then that would be a far greater victory for the scientific spirit than we have any reason to expect. Such unanimity is not to be found in any branch of human inquiry'.[60] The important thing for history, Passmore notes, is 'that there are regular ways of settling issues, by the use of which men of whatever party can be brought to see what actually happened'.[61] This same issue is at stake in moral inquiry: Can one hope to achieve agreement by rational means, or are moral differences, in principle, interminable? I shall argue for the former alternative, but at the present stage of the argument all one can say is that moral judgements make a claim to interpersonal validity and, by virtue of this claim, give grounds for hope that one can find interpersonal agreement.

These grounds are that individual perplexity has some obvious logical similarities to interpersonal disagreement (for example, we talk of being 'of two minds' about something), and that perplexity about what is right or wrong is sometimes resolved by rational means. In other words, we all find solutions to moral problems which satisfy our standards of rationality; as I have been arguing, this implies the claim that others ought to agree with our solutions and, therefore, the belief that they could be brought to agree with these solutions if they would give due consideration to the reasons which led us to them.

The last sentence gives an indication of the second, and much more serious, sense in which it could be objected that my argument proves only that moral judgements claim to be valid for those who accept the same standards. The objector would argue, rightly, that the extension of the claim into the interpersonal realm is dependent upon my saying that moral standards are accepted as 'valid' in the sense of 'rationally binding'. This interpretation, he would say, is incorrect; when one says that moral standards are 'valid', or that one appeals to moral standards to 'justify' or 'give a reason for' a moral judgement (if one wants to use that kind of language), what one means is: 'According to my moral code this is a valid standard'; or, 'I have accepted this as a reason for saying that something is right or wrong.' Thus, one can claim that others who accept the same standards ought to agree with one's judgements, but no more.

In the first place, the interpretation of 'valid' as meaning 'valid-for-me' is saying that there is something special in this use of 'valid', not that there is something special about me. The 'existentialist' interpretation, which says that each man is *sui generis* and, therefore, *sui juris*, does not, of itself, rule out a rational justification of moral beliefs. It is based on a belief about the nature of man, not on a theory of the logic of moral discourse. Moreover, if each man's uniqueness is such that he is, in the strict sense, *sui juris*, then there is no basis for the universalisability of moral judgements, since no two people can ever be similarly situated. I shall argue below, in my second argument in favour of saying that moral judgements make a universal claim on the judgements of others, that the attempt to make each man *sui juris* without reference to his *genus* (that is, in the sense of the present objection) is equally incompatible with the principle of universalisability.

One might note, further, the similarity between this objection and the first, which said that we cannot claim that others *ought* to accept our judgements because, as a matter of fact, they *will* not. The second objection commits the same interesting version of the 'naturalistic fallacy', making the normative claim dependent upon the factual acceptance. I have been arguing in line with the principle of universalisability that, if I say that I ought to accept certain standards, then I am committed to saying that others ought to accept them, and the objector has replied by denying that I *ought* to accept them; it is merely that I *do* accept them.

Finally, the valid-for-me interpretation of moral standards is incompatible with some points that have already been established: (a) Since there is a distinctive moral point of view, moral concepts reveal similarities between different actions which could not otherwise be detected. Moral inquiry is a conceptual activity; it is a way of understanding and interpreting human behaviour. Such an activity cannot be explained as the acceptance of standards solely for the guidance of one's own actions, for the acknowledgement of similarity, as we have seen, makes an interpersonal claim. (b) Without this cognitive activity, there would be no relevant types of action and, thus, no policies that one could decide to adopt. (c) At least some moral standards are such that they require that reasons be given to justify the performance of certain types of action. Moral standards are like logical standards of argument. When I say that an argument does not carry conviction, I am saying more than that it does not convince *me*. I am saying that it ought not to convince *anyone* because it is not a good argument. Similarly, when I say that the desire to take a man's lamb (or his wife) is not a good reason for taking his life, I am not saying that it is not a good reason for *me*. I am saying that it is not a good reason for *anyone*, and anyone ought to acknowledge it. (d) At least some moral standards are rules for the use of moral terms of the type that we follow these rules without being able to state them. The acceptance of such rules cannot be the result of deliberate decision in the way that axiom-choice and definition stipulation can be. (e) The valid-for-me thesis cannot sensibly be combined with the principle of universalisability for the following reason. Since similarity between actions is determined by the relevant moral standard, to say that this standard is the product of one's own choice is to say that the similarity between actions is as well. 'Judge like cases alike!' is a pointless injunction to impose upon someone who has the right to decide which cases are alike.

There is a third sense in which we could take the objection that my argument proves only that moral judgements make a claim on the judgements of those who accept the same standards. In this sense, the objector is saying that there are no grounds for choosing between different sets of standards. Since moral standards are embodied within a system of concepts which operates in accordance with its own set of rules, people who have different standards are following a different set of rules; that is, they are playing different 'language games'. To claim that one's moral standards are valid for other people is like trying to get people to play chess in accordance with the rules of football.

There is much about this position which is true and important. It is important, for example, to realise that differences in the appraisal of individual actions generally (not always, since they may result from factual error) indicate differences, perhaps even radical differences, in the conceptual schemata within which judgements were made. This is why it is so easy for those who wish to make the point to prove that moral judgements cannot be derived from the facts of a case. There can be no fruitful discussion of individual cases between people who are employing different conceptual schemata, except, perhaps, as indicators of each other's position, because they are speaking different languages. If they are to come to terms with each other, it can only be by tracing their differences back to the point of departure which is the source of their differences in particular appraisals. The sense of the present objection is that there is no point of departure, since this would presume a point of agreement and, thus, the grounds for the resolving of differences. One of my chief projects will be to show that this view is mistaken. For the present, it will be sufficient to show that the 'language game' objection rests on questionable grounds because the analogy with different games does not seem to apply to moral differences.

One can easily think of cases in which two sets of standards are applied in the appraisal of the same action and in which the language game model is clearly applicable. For example, one can speak of a 'clever theft'. The act, that is, is being commended by technical standards and condemned by moral standards. It would not make sense to ask which is the *correct* set of standards to apply to this action, or whether the act is *really* to be commended or condemned, because it is commendable according to the rules of one language game and condemnable by the rules of the other; one must decide which language game one is playing. To ask these senseless questions is like asking whether a red car is *really* 'red' or a 'car'.

The difference between this sort of category mistake and the question, whether one can find grounds for choosing between different sets of moral standards, is clear: in the 'clever theft' example both sets of standards can be accepted and consistently applied to the same act by the same appraiser, whereas in the case of conflicting moral standards this cannot be done. To ask whether an act is right or wrong is not like asking whether an object is red or a car, but like asking whether it is a car or a tree.

People who have different standards are not playing different language games in the same sense in which the 'technical game' is different from the 'moral game' in the appraisal of thefts, or in the sense in which chess is different from football. They are following different rules (e. g., they designate different things as 'right'), and it is permissible to say that this is sufficient to warrant calling the language games they are playing different games, but in another sense they are playing the same game. It is as if one team were following the rules of rugby and the other of American football, but that they were playing on the same field with the same ball, or similarly with chess and draughts. They are playing the same game because the different sets of rules do not bypass one another; they are in conflict with each other.

Since the important feature about conflicting moral standards is that one cannot consistently apply them in the appraisal of the same act, it will be helpful to consider the type of situation in which this confrontation takes place. There is no need for extensive travel in order to encounter different moral standards; these conflicts arise between people living together in the same society, and even within an individual person. For example, there is widespread disagreement in our present society about the morality of abortion and of euthanasia. Many people have definite views one way or the other about these issues, but there are also many who are in a state of confusion which reflects the public dispute. In fact, the perplexity which these people feel, torn between conflicting moral standards, is a typical example of the perplexity engendered by all moral problems.

Whenever someone wonders what he ought to do it is because there seem to be good reasons for saying that a proposed course of action is right and for saying that it is wrong; that is, there is a conflict of standards. One thinks of the old problem alluded to earlier, about whether it is right to deceive a potential murderer and of Sartre's famous dilemma about the conflicting claims of family and country.[62] Kemp provides us with a good example which brings out the fact that a conflict of moral standards is different from a case of opposite appraisals made from different points of view, as in the 'clever theft' example. 'An action may, as Locke says, deserve death in that it is a case of murder; another may deserve praise or reward in that it is a case of kind-heartedness or public-spiritedness. But what if the same action is both at once? How, for example, does one decide what is the proper attitude to adopt to a mother who deliberately kills her child because it is suffering from a painful and incurable disease?'[63] Kemp points out that one cannot deal with this, as one can with a clever theft, by assessing the action differently from different points of view: 'It is no use saying that *qua* murder the act is wrong and *qua* kind-heartedness it is right.'[64] Since both standards cannot be consistently applied, one must decide which is the correct standard.

Moral dilemmas of this type are logically similar to the problems raised in saying that moral judgements make a universal claim on the judgements of others. As I have said, this claim follows from the belief that one has applied a valid standard correctly. To object that others subscribe to different standards is to say that this claim is met by counter-claims which, if the agent is aware of them, he must take into account before he can pronounce that a proposed course of action is right or wrong, for he cannot think that he is applying the appropriate norm unless he can satisfy himself that the conflicting claims are not justified. This consideration of opposing claims and counter-claims, when the latter arise from standards proposed by someone else, is the same sort of inquiry as that in which the conflicting standards are among those one has previously acknowledged as valid. In both cases, one is faced with reasons for saying that something is right and for saying that it is wrong, and one must decide which set of reasons is to be preferred.

Moral dilemmas can be excruciatingly difficult, even insoluble in practice. I shall say more about them later in my discussion of the method of ethical argument. For now, I want to point out that we do frequently solve them. Some people are satisfied with the arguments on one side or the other about the morality of abortion and euthanasia. In the classic dilemma, Kant was able to decide that one would be wrong to deceive a potential murderer on the grounds that one could not will lying to be a universal law; Kovesi has recently decided it the other way by defining a class of actions called 'saving-deceit' which is distinguished from lying in the same way (logically, that is, not morally) as threats are distinguished from promises.[65] I am not concerned here with the validity of these conclusions, but with the fact that one is not necessarily stymied when confronted with conflicting standards. Kant and Kovesi, as examples, have found what they thought were reasonable grounds for settling one such conflict. That they decided it differently is interesting, but beside the present point, which is that rational discussion does not end with the discovery that there is a conflict of standards. These philosophers have given reasons for their respective conclusions; there is something that one can sensibly argue about, which was not the case when the different standards were part of different language games, as in the 'clever theft' example. It is true that this sort of conflict in standards is settled by appeal to the agent's system of moral beliefs and that this is not possible when the conflicting standards come from different systems. However, it is also true that people are sometimes persuaded to modify their standards by the arguments of others, which means that it is possible to find interpersonal grounds for choosing between conflicting standards.

One must resist the temptation, at this stage, to leap to the question of the ultimate justification of moral judgements. The purpose of the present argument was merely to rebut the objection that moral judgements cannot claim validity for those who subscribe to different standards because standards are operative within mutually independent language games. The objection is unfounded because: (a) the 'games' in question are not mutually independent, but are competing on the same grounds; and (b) one can find a point of view from which one can sensibly argue the merits of conflicting standards, even when these standards are proposed by different people.

There is, as I have mentioned, a second argument to prove that the universality of extension, which requires that we judge like cases alike, presupposes a universal claim on other people's judgements, which asserts that anyone ought to agree that what we think to be right is right. This follows from the fact of universalisation: if one thinks that anyone similarly situated ought to act as one ought to act, then one thinks that anyone ought to agree that this is the right course of action. Otherwise it would appear that one was saying that people ought to do what they did not think was the right thing to do. This cannot be countered by the objection that the principle of universalisability consists, not in legislation for others, but in assuring the logical consistency of one's own judgements, because the latter amounts to a type of legislation for others.

It is not, of course, that one would want to call in the police to enforce one's moral opinions, nor even that one need feel that one ought to try to persuade others to accept one's opinions. However, logical consistency does demand that one judge the actions of others by the same standards as those by which one judges one's own actions, which means that one has an opinion about what other people ought to do, given the requisite similarity, and that, if one is asked for one's honest opinion, one will say what one thinks the other person ought to do. This implies that the other ought to accept the standard in accordance with which the judgement was made as a valid reason for saying that the recommended course of action is right, for otherwise there would be no reason for saying that he ought to do it, and one is unjustified in saying that he ought to do it; which is to say, one cannot judge like cases alike.

In other words, if Jones is in a situation which is, in all relevant respects, similar to a case in which one has decided that X was the right course of action, and if Jones is, in all relevant respects, like oneself, then one is obliged to judge that Jones ought to do X. But 'Jones ought to do X' implies that Jones ought to agree that X is right. Let us suppose, for example, that Jones thinks that X is wrong. One could not say, 'Jones ought to do X even though he thinks that it is wrong', for this would commit one to the universal statement that people ought to do what they think is wrong. Either one thinks that Jones should change his mind about X (which is what I have been arguing) or one does not think that Jones ought to do X (which *ex hypothesi* one does think he ought to do). Thus, the principle of universalisability implies that moral judgements make a universal claim on other people's judgements.

This argument could be formalised in the following fashion: Let U stand for the principle of universalisability; P for the principle that one ought not to do what one thinks is wrong; S for 'I ought to do X'; T for 'Jones ought to do X'; J for 'Jones thinks that X is wrong'. Let us also presume that there is the requisite similarity for U to be applicable. Now it is clear that U combined with S yields T and that P combined with J yields not-T. In order to avoid this inconsistency, one would have to change the value of one of the propositions in the premises. *Ex hypothesi* one does not want to give up U or S. Therefore, one must either give up P or one must think that J should be changed to not-J; but the latter is the same as to say that one thinks that Jones should change his mind.

There is admittedly much that needs to be worked out (and not all of it logical) about the relation between statements of the form, 'A thinks he ought to do X', and those of the form, 'A ought to do X'. This topic, apart from the simple logical point made above, is outside the scope of the present study. Nevertheless, one might guard against a possible misinterpretation of what has been said. The above argument does not support a conclusion such as: 'Nazis think it is right to kill Jews; therefore Nazis ought to kill Jews.' To think that 'If A ought to do X, he ought to think that X is right' is equivalent to 'If A thinks that X is right, he ought to do X' is to be trapped by an elementary logical confusion.

In the preceding arguments, the claim of moral judgements to interpersonal validity is a consequence of the cognitivity of ethics. This is the reverse of the naturalistic approach which attempts to show that, because moral judgements can be inferred from interpersonally acceptable morally neutral premisses, ethics is cognitive. In other words, I agree with, and have given reasons which strengthen, the critique of naturalism which says that a close inspection of the attempted inferences reveals that a moral premiss has been implicitly introduced. However, the latter contention is the opposite of a denial of the cognitivity of ethics. It is something like saying that a close inspection of any attempt to infer physical-object statements from premisses which contain only statements about observable properties will reveal that physical-object concepts have been tacitly employed.

Any attempt to make a formal derivation of statements in a universe of discourse (U) from statements in another universe of discourse (V) is an attempt to reduce U to V; that is, it is an attempt to show that U is not an autonomous universe of discourse. I have argued, not only that such a reduction is not possible with regard to ethics, but that the employment of ethical concepts requires special cognitive activity over and above the understanding of the relevant factual and logical considerations. It is a necessary condition for the use of a word like 'murder' that one be able to apply it to the appropriate instances, which means that one must be able to identify similar cases. This similarity can be detected only if one knows why the type of action called 'murder' is wrong. Such a claim to understanding can, of course, be mistaken, but part of what is meant by saying 'I understand' is that anyone else who considered the case properly should come to the same understanding.

There is no question but that we need an analysis of how we form our moral concepts. Such an analysis will not be attempted in the present work, but that does not invalidate what has already been said. In the first place, it is surely a necessary step towards an adequate analysis that one correctly identify what is to be analysed. Further, we have no analysis of the type required for any other kind of concept. Finally, my conclusion that moral judgements are cognitive and make interpersonal claims followed from an investigation of the conditions which are necessary to explain the way we actually use moral terms. If this conclusion is incorrect it is because I misrepresented or misunderstood the way we use moral terms, not because I have not carried the analysis any further. As has been mentioned, the *a priori* claim that the use of moral terms does not require the same sort of understanding as is required for the use of other kinds of terms exhibits a prejudicial attitude in favour of the non-cognitivity of ethics and applies different standards to ethics from those which are applied to any other discipline.

In Part Two I shall study the way that the interpersonal claim of moral judgements is defended in ethical argument and, in particular, will take up the question of whether ethical disagreements can be settled in principle.

Part Two

The Method of Ethical Inquiry

18. *The Need for Method*

If moral judgements are cognitive and claim interpersonal validity, we ought to be able to reach rational solutions to moral problems and to resolve ethical disagreements. This suggests certain other general, and more fundamental, questions: e.g., when is a claim justified? or, when can we say that the solution of a problem has been found? In general, what we would appear to need is the statement of criteria which must be met if a proposed answer is to be an adequate solution to the problem and, therefore, to justify the claim that others ought to agree. Then we could test ethical statements in accordance with these critera in order to see whether or not they 'measure up'.

This technique has been applied frequently in the recent past – most notoriously in Ayer's *Language, Truth and Logic*[1] – and, almost invariably, moral discourse has failed to pass muster. In his noteworthy article, 'The Lesbian Rule', Lucas summarises the problem:

> The thesis can be restated as the claim that value words carry with them an undertaking to justify if required. Words then like 'true', 'right', 'valid', 'cause', 'consequence', would all mean 'conclusively provable', and might legitimately be used only if there is a decision procedure available, whether of observation or scientific experiment, truth table analysis, or a chain of incontestable deductive steps.[2]

Clearly, deductive proof is the only one of the 'decision procedures' which is even likely to be of any use in the attempt to justify moral judgements. Accordingly, Lucas points out that what is being required is that the moral agent have a system of rules from which he could deduce all and only the proper conclusions and by means of which, therefore, 'he could conclusively establish his correctitude' when he says, for example, that he 'ought' to do something. Lucas goes on to argue, as we shall see later, that it is a mistake to construe moral discourse on the model of a deductive system. What he does not mention (because it is irrelevant to the point he is making) is that, if we do so construe it, we are faced with a special problem because a deductive proof must consist of a finite number of steps. Thus, the system is based on a set of ultimate principles or axioms which, if the conclusions derived from them are to claim interpersonal validity, must themselves be valid. The special difficulty is that, since these principles are ultimate, one has *ex hypothesi* exhausted one's supply of moral reasons. So if the axioms are to be valid, they must either be self-evidently so or be validated from outside the system, which is to say, they must be derived from morally neutral propositions. The well-documented weaknesses of intuitionism and naturalism have provided powerful arguments for saying that the ultimate principles cannot be validated and, therefore, that moral judgements make no interpersonal claims.

There are some quite obvious difficulties that beset any attempt, like that outlined in the last paragraph, to lay down beforehand a list of strict requirements for entry into the realm of rational discourse: (a) When one closes the door against undesirables, one might well find that one has also locked out some old friends. I shall show later that the methods which have been employed to disqualify moral discourse do in fact exclude a wide range of apparently respectable expressions. (b) The attempt may be self-defeating. It is well-known that the principle which requires that statements be confirmed by observation or deductive proof cannot itself be validated by either. (c) More important, and fundamental, is the fact that it would seem to be all but impossible to make an exhaustive list of the possible ways in which statements may be justified. Not only would this seem to require the demonstration of a universal negative, but it is difficult to see how it could be constructed with sufficient flexibility to account for such a complex activity as human thought. For example, Lucas responds to the not uncommon position quoted in the last paragraph by producing the counter-example of a judge deciding a point of law. His judgement is not reached by the simple application of a clear rule (if it could have been so decided, it would not have been a disputed point), but, on the other hand, neither is his judgement arbitrary. 'There is thus not an exhaustive disjunction between being in accordance with some definite rule and being completely unruly, between the conclusively justified and the quite unjustified.'[3]

In an article to which I have already referred, Passmore considers a more extended list of criteria, ranging in diminishing severity from the 'Cartesian' demands exemplified in the position examined by Lucas to the requirement that conclusions be reached which are 'universally acceptable'.[4] He concludes that all we can demand of a branch of inquiry is that there be 'regular ways of settling issues'.[5] D. Pole takes a similarly flexible approach, finding in the very possibility of agreement some measure of guarantee for the validity of the conclusions reached: 'Once we are collectively launched on the current of rational inquiry, the process in some measure takes over; the workings of individual minds are involved in the course of a larger movement whose direction is never wholly predictable. We call reason 'objective' in this sense: without talking nonsense we cannot describe ourselves as choosing what views shall emerge from a genuine inquiry – views which we shall adopt and advocate as "rational".'[6]

Therefore, rather than state *a priori* the conditions which must be met if the logical claim made by moral judgements is justified, I shall approach the problem from the other direction. Since one's moral judgements claim that others ought to agree with them, let us seek for some method by which this agreement can be reached.

19.   *The Claim Provides the Method*

In order to test a claim, it is necessary, first of all, to discover what is being claimed, and this information, conversely, provides the clue which solves the problem of how to go about conducting the test. We would not, for example, test a man's claim to be the strongest man in the world by getting him to recite Virgil; nor would a court of law accept conclusive proof that the plaintiff was married as evidence for or against his claim to have been injured in a car accident. This seems nothing but common sense, yet it is no exaggeration to say that one of the chief discoveries which led to the rapid advance of science was the realisation that the claims made by scientists could be tested by certain quantitative methods; and it is an unfortunate fact of history that many have misunderstood the significance of this discovery, thinking that the method which proved to be so successful in testing one type of claim should be appropriate to all claims which are not purely formal. This, of course, is not the case.

The claim made by a moral judgement is that it is the correct solution to a moral problem, that it answers the question of whether a course of action is right or wrong. We can understand the nature of the claim more clearly by recalling the typical structure of a moral problem. As I have already indicated, moral problems do not exist independently of perplexed people. When a person is perplexed about whether something is right or wrong it is because he thinks that there might be some reason for saying that it is right or wrong. Thus, in order to understand the problem (and the proposed solution) we must first know why there is thought to be a problem. In general we can say that when someone wonders whether an action is right or wrong it is because he suspects that it is of a type which is required or forbidden by his moral standards. A man who has no moral standards regarding a certain type of action has no moral problems in that respect, as we saw was the situation of a completely secularised man *vis-à-vis* sacrilege. (Section 14 above.) If someone had no moral standards, he would have no moral problems. We saw further that, given a moral problem, not only could we not hope for a solution, but we could not sensibly inaugurate an inquiry outside a context established by a moral concept since, in such an instance, facts would be neither relevant nor irrelevant, but meaningless. (Section 7 above.) This led to a comparison of moral inquiry with scientific inquiry in which facts are collected with reference to some hypothesis; the hypothesis in a moral inquiry is that the course of action under discussion is right or wrong because it is a member of a class of actions governed by a moral concept. These considerations indicate the type of method which is appropriate for conducting moral arguments and, therefore, for testing proposed solutions to moral problems.

The concepts which define types of action for the purpose of moral judgement, like other concepts, provide a *rationale* for the identification of individual cases; that is, for the use of the appropriate term, when it is the case that we have a term. (Section 14 above.) Since moral problems arise when one wonders whether or not a course of action is of a type defined by a moral concept, this question can only be settled by reference to, and, if necessary, by clarification of, the guiding *rationale*. This is the basic structure of moral inquiry. We are provided with a good model of this kind of investigation by the legal procedure in a murder trial. The law, as represented and interpreted by the judge, determines what is to count as murder, what evidence is admissible, what facts are to be considered as relevant; it is the function of the jury to consider the factual evidence and, in the light of the judicial interpretation, to pronounce the final verdict. If a question arises, not about what the facts are, but about what the facts amount to, it must be referred back to the judge for clarification. In a moral inquiry we have a similar dialectic between the moral concept and the case under consideration. If X is a moral term, the verdict which is sought is that a course of action is right or wrong because it is a case of X.

One interesting corollary is that it is not the case, as is sometimes alleged, that we are always more certain of the facts than we are of their interpretation. In general, one would not even know what facts to look for except under the guidance of an accepted moral standard. There is no way to attribute sense to the contention that one can approach situations with no moral preconceptions and by a mere consideration of the facts come to the conclusion (whether by derivation or decision) that one ought to do something. For one thing, moral problems are not suggested by brute facts. For another, there is no limit to the number of circumstances and consequences that may, or may not, enter into the structure of a 'situation'; any selection, weighting, ascription of relevance – in short, any consideration of the facts – must be done in the light of moral preconceptions.

It might be objected that the method of inquiry which I have outlined is both too simple and too restrictive to accommodate such a complex and diversified activity as is exhibited in moral discourse. The only adequate reply is a plea for patience. As we work out the method in more detail, we shall see that it incorporates a great deal more complexity than might appear on the surface. It is true, in reply to the second point, that I am restricting the discussion, for the present, to one type of moral problem; namely, the sort of problem that is presented when the rightness of a particular course of action is in question. However, it would appear to be a matter of some value if the method can adequately deal with this most common and fundamental type of problem. Moreover, some types of problems (e. g., the choice of the better, or the less evil, of two alternatives and the settling of conflicts of principle) are clearly no more than permutations or complications of this basic type, and other moral considerations, which are not directly concerned with the right choice of action, do nevertheless have a bearing on that choice and, to that extent, will come under our purview. The most serious of the apparent difficulties is how, if it is claimed that moral problems arise only in relation to already accepted standards, one is to account for the acceptance or modification of standards. The answer to this will become more clear as we proceed, but is briefly this: When it is not merely a question of facts, problematic cases arise on the peripheries of moral concepts as questions about the correct extension of these concepts; e.g., one is not perplexed about the morality of killing a bank clerk in the course of an armed robbery, but one is perplexed about certain cases of euthanasia. When such a case has been decided, it becomes, by virtue of the principle of universalisability, the paradigm of a new type (either assimilated as a sub-type or distinguished from the original classification) and thus incorporates a moral standard, which is, depending upon how the case was settled, either a modification (or clarification) of the original standard or a new standard. Thus moral judgements involve, at least implicitly, judgements about standards, or 'decisions of principle', but always in relation to presently held standards, without which the problem would never have arisen. One acquires new moral concepts, as one learns new words in general, by defining them in relation to, and incorporating them into, one's present conceptual scheme. The point is that the method which I am proposing does deal with the problem of accepting and modifying moral standards. Even the standards which are already accepted as valid can be subjected to criticism, but only in terms of other standards, since to call a moral concept into question is to render the corresponding type of action problematic, and this problem can be dealt with in the same fashion as were others. My position does not require an inflexibility of moral standards chiefly because of the open-texture of moral terms; one's scheme of moral concepts is not a rigid framework, like a number system which remains unchanged by application, but is constantly being adjusted as questions arise about the limits of extension.[7]

One question which remains intractable is that about the 'foundation' of ethics. The moral problems which I have been envisaging all arise within an already established, however rudimentary, system of values. But what of the *first* moral problem? How does the 'moral point of view' suggest itself to someone who has no stock of moral concepts? What is the basis of the moral enterprise? This is the sort of question that philosophers typically ask, sometimes in the form of an inquiry into the meaning of 'good', 'right', or 'ought'. As was the case when it came to stating the criteria which must be met if a claim is to be justified, I am suggesting a more modest approach to the problem. The search for 'foundations' presupposes an edifice; the theorist axiomatises an existing practice. Let us then, rather than make one more attempt to force moral discourse into *a priori* categories, examine how people can, and do, reach agreement on moral categories, and try to discover what considerations underlie their reasoning. Without promising to solve the problem of the 'basis of ethics', one can hope at least to raise some relevant questions and to point to the direction in which a solution may be expected to be found.

20. *Consistency and Deduction*

If ethical inquiry typically consists in the attempt to decide whether or not a particular action is of a type defined by a moral concept, one is tempted to accept as a model a form of conceptual subsumption in which the elements are selected in accordance with a clear-cut *rationale*. A likely example is provided by 'rectangle' which denotes a quadrilateral with four right angles. If one is unsure whether a figure is a rectangle, one inspects it in the light of the requirements set out by the definition of 'rectangle' and readily decides the issue. The procedure is, indeed, correct, but the choice of 'rectangle', which is not an open-textured term, is misleading. The judgement, 'This is a rectangle', can be derived from the definition of 'rectangle' combined with a premiss stating that the figure in question has four straight sides enclosing right angles. We shall see later that, not only moral judgements, but denotative statements in general are not susceptible of a strict deductive proof of this kind. Moreover, as has been indicated, the attempt to construe moral reasoning on the model of a deductive system easily leads into a cul-de-sac. Fortunately Lucas has provided us with a way out by constructing an elegant argument to show that deduction from clear rules is not the only way to arrive at rational conclusions – indeed, that it is not the only way to proceed *more geometrico*.[8] I shall follow his argument in some detail before bringing it into line with the present discussion.

Lucas sets out by contrasting two methods of argumentation:

> . . . The first dialogue exemplifies Kant's canon 'Act only on the maxim which you can at the same time will that it should become a universal law'. Two professors, the Professor of Ethiopian Language and Culture and the Professor of Comparative Education, are talking over the port. The Professor of Ethiopian Language and Culture leads off:
>
> 'You ought to live within $4\frac{1}{2}$ miles of Carfax, you know.'
> 'Why?', says the Professor of Comparative Education.
> 'All professors should.'

'All professors! What about you? Bibury is more than $4\frac{1}{2}$ miles from Carfax, you know.'

'Ah, when I said "All professors", I was speaking broadly: I meant "All professors who profess soft-option subjects have to live within $4\frac{1}{2}$ miles from Carfax." Ethiopian Language and Culture, as you are aware, is an autonomous discipline with standards all its own; so the ruling does not apply to me.'

'I see; but what about the Professor of Experimental Theology? You would call that a soft-option subject, I suppose, yet he lives at Stanton-in-the-Vale.'

'I ought to have been more precise still. It is only those professors holding soft-option chairs who are not obliged to indulge in experiments who have to live within the radius. . . .'

In this dialogue the structure is clear; every singular judgement, such as 'You ought to live within $4\frac{1}{2}$ miles of Carfax', must be subsumed under some universal principle, some open rule; the onus is upon the proponent of the singular judgement to set forth this rule in a satisfactory and acceptable way, and it is open to his adversary, the disputant, to show that the rule as he formulates it does not cover exactly the case required. The second dialogue which I now shall exhibit differs in that no subsumption under a universal principle is attempted and that the onus of proof is differently disposed. It might go thus, the Professor of Ethiopian Language and Culture starting:

'You ought to live within $4\frac{1}{2}$ miles of Carfax.'

'Why?', retorts the Professor of Comparative Education. 'What about you?'

'Ah, yes, but my case is different. You profess a soft-option subject, whereas I don't.'

'Well, what about the Professor of Experimental Theology?'

'Ah, but his case is different too; he does experiments.'

'Well, what about . . .' – and so on.[9]

The difference between these two models is that *onus probandi* is placed, in the first case, on the proponent; in the second, on the disputant. In the first, the proponent must enunciate a principle which will serve as a major premiss from which it is possible to deduce all and only those conclusions which it is desired to justify; in the second he is merely required to account for apparent discrepancies:

> Instead of the canon which regulates the first dialogue 'In such and such circumstances one ought always to act thus and thus' we have the much more accommodating one 'one ought always to act similarly in circumstances which are sufficiently similar or, as I might put it, which sufficiently closely resemble one another.' [10]

It is, Lucas contends, the second model which represents the logical character of ethical discourse:

> ... [The] second dialogue is the one that correctly exhibits our logical commitments. What has happened so often in ethics is that philosophers, sensing the requirement of consistency which the use of value words enjoins on us, have formulated that requirement in the shape of some law of universality which, as it stands, cannot hold. They have made an unconscious and illegitimate transition from the second dialogue to the first, and have been led by this confusion to look for an impossible rigour in ethical rules. [11]

Lucas then goes on to show the structural similarity between the second type of dialogue and the method of taking a limit by means of the *delta-epsilon* notation:

> The point is that when I announce that $f(x)$ approaches a limit $f(x_0)$ as x approaches x_0, I do *not* mean that I can specify a degree of closeness of x to x_0 which will make $f(x)$ approach $f(x_0)$ as near as you please; that is to say I do *not* claim that I can specify a degree of closeness of x to x_0 such that you cannot find objection to it. I make instead the weaker claim that if you first specify your requirements of how close $f(x)$ is to be to $f(x_0)$, I will *then* find a degree of closeness of x to x_0 such that your requirement is satisfied. [12]

This leads to the suggestion that 'if only we were able to construe the connexions of humanist reasoning as *functions* we might be able to apply the procedure of mathematical analysis and exhibit the rules of reasoning as part of the theory of functions',[13] and thence the interpretation of the relation of a moral situation to the response to that situation as a functional relationship 'such that given any possible moral situation, which we take to be the argument of the function, there is determined one and only one correct response, which is the value of the given function.'[14] It becomes clear then that the second conversation resembles the taking of a limit since the standards of similarity are first stated with regard to the responses (i. e., the values of the function) and then it is shown that there is a corresponding similarity (or dissimilarity) in the respective situations (i. e., the arguments): 'which is to say, however stringent a standard of closeness of resemblance is chosen for the responses it is possible to find a standard of closeness of resemblance for the original situations such that if any situation is sufficiently close by the latter standard its response will also be sufficiently close by the former standard'.[15] By the use of this mathematical analogy, Lucas is able to show that the requirements in the second form of dialogue are similar to the requirements for a *continuous* function, whereas those in the first form resemble the requirements for a *constant* function, which is more than we require.

There obviously will be points at which the analogy does not fit. One of the more important is that numerical 'closeness' is easy to understand, but moral 'closeness', especially with respect to responses, is not. Lucas gets round this neatly by redefining continuity of function in terms of 'open class' rather than of 'neighbourhood'. The logical claim now reads: 'however stringent are the criteria for a response's being similar to another given one, if some situation evokes a response which according to those criteria is dissimilar, then there exists an open class of which this situation is not, and the original situation was, a member'.[16] Another problem, and one which Lucas admits is intractable by his method, is that of relevance. 'This is because questions of relevance are material questions while consistency is only a formal requirement.'[17] I shall now take up the question of how relevance can be accommodated.

21. *From Form to Matter*

What Lucas has provided us with, one could fairly say, is a quite valuable gloss on the principle of universalisability. He has, that is, helped us to see more clearly what is involved in saying that we must judge like cases alike. However, just as the injunction to be consistent does not enable us to tell which cases are alike, his sophisticated method for testing consistency leaves us needing a way to identify the appropriate open classes. Fortunately, since Lucas has given an example of how this method of argumentation would work in practice, we can look again at the imaginary dispute for a clue as to how the necessary material questions are settled.

One can be made uneasy, upon comparing the two arguments, by the fact that the moves in the second argument appear to be guided by the very principles which were explicitly stated in the first; indeed, without the first, it would not have been so easy to make sense of the second. One wonders why the disputant, rather than asking: 'Why? what about you?' and 'What about the Professor of Experimental Theology?', had not instead asked: 'What about Mao Tse-tung? or my next-door neighbour?' Perhaps the most sensible question would have been, simply, 'Why?'; surely there are very few people who would not be completely disarmed if they were taken to task for not living within $4\frac{1}{2}$ miles of Carfax. It is clear that underlying the argument is the belief, on the part of the Professor of Ethiopian Culture, that there is a class of people who ought to live within $4\frac{1}{2}$ miles of Carfax and, on the part of the Professor of Comparative Education, both the realisation that his colleague has this belief and some notion of the *rationale* by which he determines who are to be counted as members of this class. Without these minimum conditions, the dialogue would have been impossible.

In spite of the difference of approach manifested in the two arguments (which difference will be considered in the next section), they have the common purpose of accrediting membership in the class of those who are bound by a residence requirement. In other words, the aim of both arguments is to define the boundary of that class; or one could transpose this into a linguistic question by coining the term

'C-resident' to designate those who are obliged to live within $4\frac{1}{2}$ miles of Carfax and seeing the problem as one about the correct use of that term. Whichever way we put it, the point is clear: questions of relevance are settled by reference to the concept; i. e., in the light of the *rationale* behind the use of 'C-resident'. Thus, the sort of inquiry envisaged by Lucas is of the standard structure; it proceeds under the guidance of a moral concept and seeks to discover whether or not that concept extends to a questionable case. What features of the case are to count as relevant and important are determined by the concept. Even more, it is only by relying on the concept that one knows what features to look for, that one can choose cases which can sensibly serve as examples or counter-examples.

All of this seems obvious enough, but it confronts us with the anomaly that the Professor of Comparative Education both understood the concept (as manifested in his ability to propose the right sort of people as counter-examples) and was aware of all the relevant facts, but still made mistakes (or, at least, disagreed) about who were to be counted as members of the class in question. The explanation, of course, is that he was aware of the relevant facts, but did not understand their relevance. This is similar to the jury having questions, not about the facts, but about what the facts amount to, and needing to refer them back to the judge; or like a person not knowing that squares must be equilateral and confusing squares with other rectangles. What is required is conceptual clarification. However, it is not so easy with moral concepts as it is with 'square' because moral concepts do not provide us with a finite list of relevant features that we are to look for in identifying specimens. The type of argument described by Lucas has the merit of equipping us to deal with questions of relevance indefinitely, but it places upon our conceptual resources the burden of enabling us, not only to recognise the presence of relevant facts (as, for example, the definition of 'square' enables us to distinguish squares from other rectangles because of the equality of the sides), but also to validate the relevance of unprecedented features.

One might note in passing that the fact that 'C-resident' denotes the type of person rather than a type of action does not serve to differentiate the type of argument described by

Lucas from my model of moral inquiry. What is at stake in his example is the question whether a course of action is right because it is of a certain type. It is sometimes the case, as in this example, that part of the definition of a type of action (or, if you will, part of the similarity between like cases) is that the agent is a certain kind of person. To take a more realistic example, moral problems sometimes arise because the agent wonders whether he is enjoined to perform some action as part of his duties as a father. Generally, the agent knows that he has such duties but questions whether *this* is one of them. However, questions can also arise about the precise extent of the concept 'father' as it occurs in this context. Surely, 'physical paternity' is not an adequate characterisation since sometimes people who are not progenitors must act *in loco parentis* and sometimes physical fathers do not have the duties of fathers. Clearly, it must be shown that a person has a duty before he can be enjoined to perform it.

22. *Consistency, Flexibility and Open-Texture*

We noticed that in the example of the method of argument recommended by Lucas the same principles were implicitly followed which were explicitly stated in the rejected argument. What are we to make of this? Are we indebted to Lucas for exhibiting this model of ethical reasoning and, as it were, clothing it with respectability by assimilating it to a type of mathematical reasoning? Or should we accuse him of canonising procrastination and muddle-headedness? To see why the first is the correct response will also be to gain a better understanding of the nature of ethical inquiry.

There is an attractive clear-headedness and straight-forwardness, as well as a *prima-facie* plausibility, in the following position: *It is the responsibility of a moral agent to be as precise as he can about the content of his moral judgements; that is, about the exact description according to which he is saying that something is right or wrong. Consistency requires no more, and no less, than that he apply the same moral label to everything which fits that description. If he later decides that he wants to make some exceptions or to extend his description, which is perfectly understandable considering the complexity of human situations, then let him honestly admit that he is changing his mind and adopting a different principle.*

One would want to endorse this call for clarity and candour without at the same time accepting the notion of consistency which accompanies it, and this surely is what Lucas was getting at. One simply cannot interpret the logical requirement of consistency to mean that the moral agent is committed to a similar judgement in all and only those cases which fit a description that he has given to a particular case. There are (at least) two arguments against this notion of consistency: (a) It is incompatible with the flexibility which was required by the proposed modification of principles; and, much more importantly: (b) It is based on a misunderstanding of how language works.

Let us take the example of the man who judges that someone ought to live within $4\frac{1}{2}$ miles of Carfax because he is a professor of a soft-option subject. On this view of consistency, he is committed to the judgement that all and only professors of soft-option subjects are so obliged. Suppose that later he decided that someone else who was, say, merely a Reader also had this obligation or that, as Lucas suggested, he wanted to make an exception in the case of the Professor of Experimental Theology. How could he justify such a change in principle? Not from an inspection of facts, certainly; one could meditate for ever on the fact that someone conducts experiments without ever discovering whether he was obliged to live somewhere. Nor does his original principle warrant any exceptions. The obvious answer, and that which was implicit in the position stated above, is that the change is not warranted or unwarranted. It is up to the moral agent to make up his own mind, and to change it if he decides to, and that is all there is to it. There is no need to restate the many difficulties which we have seen to be inherent to this position, but it is important, at this point, to see that, far from being a strict demand for consistency, this amounts to a denial of such a requirement. If there is no warrant for changing principles, then there is no control over what changes might be made. The man in the example could as easily have made some extraordinary change, like saying that everybody (or nobody) ought to live within $4\frac{1}{2}$ miles of Carfax. Even the minor change that

was made involves a formal contradiction between the original·
and the modified principles. If one accepts this view of consistency, the only way to be consistent is to stick to one's
stated principles with absolute rigidity. Consistency is bought
at the price of flexibility, and vice versa. To require logical
consistency and then to allow the agent to change his principles at will is to take away with one hand what has been
given with the other.

In actual fact we can restrict and extend the application of
our moral concepts without inconsistency; indeed these
modifications can be made in order to meet the demands of
consistency. This is not to say, as it might be interpreted in the
view stated above, that *after* the changes are made, *then* we can
judge more consistently, but that consistency requires that we
make the changes, which appear as inconsistencies on the
above view. The criterion of consistency in moral judgements
is the 'sense' of these judgements, not the words with which
we, at one time or another, more or less imperfectly, express
that 'sense'. Like cases are alike, as we have seen, not because
they fit some description which we have given to a type of action, but because they are right or wrong for the same reason.
We noted earlier that the moves in the second argument
proposed by Lucas did not make sense unless one knew the
principles which were explicitly stated in the first argument; it
would be more accurate to say that neither argument made
sense unless one knew why it was that certain people were required to live within $4\frac{1}{2}$ miles of Carfax. If one is given an
adequate answer to this question, one is equipped to apply the
term 'C-resident' correctly: which is to say, one is enabled to
be consistent in one's moral judgements in this respect.

The consideration of the relationship between consistency
and flexibility has led us to the second point, viz.: that the
view that consistency is determined in accordance with stated
principles or descriptions of types of cases rests upon a mis-
conception of language. When one sees that the question of
who is obliged to live within $4\frac{1}{2}$ miles of Carfax can be treated
as a question about the correct use of 'C-resident', one ap-
preciates the value of the Lucas argument. It is not a conces-
sion to the lazy and muddle-headed, but the taking account of
the logical realities. What the first argument required was a

complete and final definition of 'C-resident', as we have for 'square' and 'rectangle', which could be coupled with a minor premiss, asserting that a particular case satisfied the necessary and sufficient conditions set out in that definition, to yield the conclusion that the person in question is a 'C-resident'. The fallacy here is that moral terms, unlike geometric terms, are 'open-textured' – which means that *one cannot state the necessary and sufficient conditions for their correct application*. If this is not obvious for the artificial example 'C-resident' (because we were not given the sense of that term), it is so for the concept 'duty of a father'. We saw some of the difficulty attendant upon defining 'father' as it is used here; it would be infinitely more difficult to give a set of rules which would enable one clearly and unmistakably to identify the particular actions which are required under that heading.

If a term cannot be given a strict definition, then one cannot justify every correct use of that term by a deductive inference, which is not to say that every use is justified. That a term has open-texture does not imply that it is applied at random. Chess, for example, is clearly a game; chess boards and chess masters certainly are not. In the article in which he coined the term 'open-texture', Waismann shows that, for such common words as 'gold', 'cat' and 'man', there is an ineradicable possibility of questionable cases.[18] He wonders: 'Suppose I come across a being that looks like a man, speaks like a man, and is only one span tall – shall I say it *is* a man?' [19] He did not, of course, suggest that the creature might be an instance of 'gold' or 'cat', for this would have been senseless. The fact that there are cases which definitely are, and others which definitely are not, members of a class, and that questionable cases are questions about the extension of one concept, or range of concepts, and definitely not about others, means that there are some limits beyond which one cannot stretch the extension of a term without destroying its sense. We are clearly justified in applying a word to the paradigm case and to those which are obviously similar to the paradigm in the relevant respects. But obvious to whom? When does the similarity cease to be obvious, and then become questionable, then contrived and strained, and finally lost altogether? What is an obvious similarity to one person might be far from that to another, even though they agree about a great number of plain cases. In such an instance, the two people are disputing about whether or not the sense of the word warrants its being applied to the case in question; or, as we might also put it, whether consistency in the use of the word requires that it be applied in this case. The Lucas argument is designed to deal with this kind of question.

23. *Settling Boundary Disputes*

Because of the nature of language, we need to be able, are able, to use words consistently when we do not have iron-clad definitions and, therefore, cannot give an incontestable proof of our consistency. However, while consistency cannot be definitively demonstrated, it can be rationally defended. If the use of a word in a given instance is 'sensible', it can be defended. Let us suppose, for example, that Jones and Smith agree that a, b and c are so-and-so's, that Jones thinks that d is a so-and-so, and that Smith thinks that it is not, and that 'so-and-so' is an open-textured term. We have here the basis for an argument, since, presumably, each has reasons for his belief about d's being a so-and-so and is thus able to defend that belief. What is important to see is that this argument is not, in principle, interminable; there are grounds upon which it might be rationally settled.

Let us first get clear about what is at stake in the argument and what, therefore, it would mean for it to be 'rationally settled'. You might say: 'The two men are merely trying to reach agreement on the meaning of a word; there are no substantial issues involved.' I shall have something to say later about the opposition between the 'merely verbal' and the 'substantial'; but, in reference to the present discussion, there are several ways in which Jones and Smith might reach agreement on the use of 'so-and-so' without having resolved their differences by rational methods. We are trying to discover what such a resolution would amount to and whether it is possible.

One way in which the two men might reach agreement is by 'agreeing to disagree'; that is, Jones would call d a so-and-so and Smith would not and they both would understand that this was the case. This is not quite as simple as it sounds, since Jones's decision to admit d into the company of so-and-so's commits him to the same judgement about any other cases (let us call them d_1, d_2 . . .) that are like d and are similarly related to a, b and c. For Jones, that is to say, d has become the paradigm for a sub-class of so-and-so's, which class of things Smith wants to distinguish from so-and-so's. Even with this, though, the two men could agree to disagree about the meaning of 'so-and-so', and, provided that there were not too many words about which they had such disagreement, their ability to communicate would not be impaired. But suppose that 'so-and-so' means 'unemployed', that d is a proper name, and that Jones and Smith are functionaries of the Ministry of Employment and Productivity whose job is to decide who is to get unemployment benefits. They could agree to disagree about whether or not d was 'unemployed', and as long as they could reach agreement as to whether or not he was entitled to unemployment benefits, this 'verbal' disagreement would not make any difference. But, surely, we would want to say that, regardless of what they say, they have reached agreement about the meaning of 'unemployed', as it is used in their context, when they have agreed about who is to get benefits.

On the other hand, the two men might agree to use the word 'so-and-so' to designate d without having reached any substantial agreement. For example, Jones might be Smith's military superior and order him to call d a so-and-so even though Smith does not agree that this is a legitimate use of the word. They will have reached agreement about the use of 'so-and-so', but Smith will believe that they have changed the sense of the word. His protest might take the following form: 'If you insist that we call this kind of hand gun a "rifle", all right, that's what we'll call it. However, I hope you realise that we shall have to change all the regulations about rifles: firing-instructions, the length of the firing-range, inspection procedures, etc.' Or, a more likely, and ominous, example would be if 'so-and-so' meant 'deserter'; to agree that d was a so-and-so would be a matter of life and death. In this case, Smith might say: 'I'll go along with calling him a "deserter" if you insist, so long as it is understood that we are not using that word in its technical sense. But what is the point? Won't

we have to find another word to refer to technical deserters?'
But suppose that Jones insisted that he meant that d was a
deserter in the strict sense of the word. Would we want to say
that Smith's acquiescence, if he were to give it, would be a
mere agreement to use the word in a certain way?

The point is that it is not always clear what is meant when
we say that people agree about the meaning of a word. What
we are looking for when we speak of Jones and Smith resolving
their differences by rational means is that they reach agreement as to whether calling d a so-and-so is consistent with the
sense of 'so-and-so' as it is used when referring to a, b and c.
There are, of course, other kinds of questions that can arise
about the meaning of 'so-and-so'; e. g. Jones and Smith might
be led by their argument to question whether 'so-and-so' is a
useful classification after all, but this question will be framed
in terms of other concepts the validity of which is not being
questioned in that inquiry. In any given linguistic transaction,
there must be some terms whose sense is not in question, but it
is nevertheless possible to question whether one of these terms
is being correctly applied in a particular instance. This is what
is at issue between Jones and Smith. 'So-and-so' has an established and mutually acceptable sense, namely, that in
which it is applied to a, b and c. They are trying to decide
whether, *in this sense*, d is also a so-and-so. Lucas has shown us
the formal mode in which such an argument is cast; the
material questions, we saw, are to be settled by reference to
the concept. What we want to know is whether such an issue
can, in principle, be settled.

As a general rule, we can say that inquiries are, in principle,
terminable, or questions decidable, if there are some 'objective' controls. This is not, as Pole has pointed out, to require
the existence of some 'object': 'We should not let etymology
constrict our thinking: objectivity, as philosophers have
sought to frame the notion, is not bound up with the presence
of an object. Even given some appropriate object we shall need
more; for our belief in the object in question will itself need to
claim objectivity. If that in turn requires the presence of an
object to make it objective, it is plain that the sequence will be
infinite.'[20] What is required is that there be some independent criterion by which competing answers can be measured;

some criterion, that is, which is not subject to the whims of Jones and Smith. We have such a criterion in the established sense of 'so-and-so'. It is not, indeed, an explicit criterion; if it were, the only questions that could arise would be factual questions, such as: Does this figure have equal sides? The criterion is implicit in the use of 'so-and-so'; it is the discoverable *rationale* behind the use of the word. We also have ample evidence to back up statements about the meaning of 'so-and-so'; namely, the whole set of acknowledged so-and-so's, which we have codified as *a*, *b* and *c*.

To say that the meaning of 'so-and-so' is not subject to deliberate change by Jones or Smith is to say more than that this meaning is the result of a social convention which no individual can, on his own account, modify. There is also a strong logical reason for saying that this meaning is 'objective'. To agree that *a*, *b* and *c* are all so-and-so's, is to agree that *a*, *b* and *c* are similar in certain, not necessarily specified, respects. Similarity between things is not something which is the subject of individual choice. One cannot, that is, sensibly say: 'I have decided that *x* and *y* are similar, and that is all there is to it!' Someone else could, with perfect propriety, ask: 'Similar in what respects?' or: 'What do they have in common?' Saying that things are similar is saying something about *them*, not about one's own choices or attitudes. It is true, of course, that sometimes one does have some choice in these matters. For example, since there is no limit to the number of ways in which *x* can be similar to other things, if one were asked to find something similar to *x*, one could produce *u*, *v*, *y*, *z*, and, in accordance with the range of one's imagination, almost anything else. In other words, if one is allowed to choose the grounds of similarity, then one can, probably, make any two things similar, provided that one is prepared to identify the respects in which they are alike. However, this move is not open to Jones or Smith. They have already agreed that what is in question is whether *d* is similar to *a*, *b* and *c* in those respects in which these things are similar to one another, and, remembering that *a*, *b* and *c* represent an open class of acknowledged so-and-so's, this is a (relatively) severe limitation.

The issue between Jones and Smith is, in principle,

decidable because there is an objective control to their inquiry. While it is true that one or both of them could stop the argument at any stage, or even refuse to discuss the question, this is beside the point. They need not. It is possible for them to reach agreement, and there is an independent measure of a correct answer. Moreover, if they do seriously discuss the question, this is already an indication of a degree of agreement, not only about a, b and c, but that d is the sort of thing that *might* be a so-and-so. To agree that there is a problem, that it is not pointless to ask whether d is a so-and-so, is already to locate d in the vaguely defined, but relatively small range of possible so-and-so's. The more severely problematic the question is, which is to say, the more difficult it is, granted complete factual knowledge, to distinguish d from the acknowledged so-and-so's, the more narrow is the range of things within which it has been located and the broader, therefore, is the agreement between Jones and Smith. Thus, the fact that the question of whether d is a so-and-so might finally be decided by imponderable factors of personal judgement does not mean that this judgement is not justified; it merely means that the judgement is not formally derived from a definition of 'so-and-so'. Before this judgement could reasonably be brought to bear, the field had to be narrowed down, by means of quite tangible and public evidence, to the relatively few things which, if not *clearly so-and-so's*, are clearly *possible* so-and-so's.

It can be objected that any inquiry which still leaves room for an element of personal judgement has not been properly terminated, because, if the solution is not incontestable, there can always be further questions raised. It is true that the judgement that d is a so-and-so, where 'so-and-so' is an open-textured term, will always be subject to questions, and its grounds capable of indefinite amplification and clarification; indeed, it is characteristic of the type of argument described by Lucas that it enables one to probe as deeply and to distinguish as precisely as one pleases without there being any absolute limit. The inquiry is terminated when agreement has been reached, but the need for personal judgement will not have been eliminated so long as there is no final statement of the necessary and sufficient conditions for a thing's being a so-and-so, which sort of statement cannot be given for an open-textured term. However, if an inquiry is in principle terminable if, and only if, it leads to strictly unquestionable conclusions, then I think it is clear that there are few, if any, types of inquiry which will qualify, and those will be of the purely formal variety. Any statement of the form, 'This is a so-and-so', where 'so-and-so' is an open-textured term, can be questioned without involving the questioner in self-contradiction.

The critical difference between the objective and the subjective, the in-principle-decidable and the undecidable, is not in whether or not one reaches unquestionable conclusions, but in whether or not one reaches conclusions on the basis of evidence which is independent of one's control. By this criterion, questions about the consistent use of open-textured terms are, in principle, decidable. The imponderable element of personal judgement that enters into the final decision is, for all that, a *judgement*, and not a choice; it claims to be an assessment of the evidence, not a product of the unfettered will. If, for example, Smith were to be persuaded by Jones's arguments and were to report: 'I have decided that *d* is a so-and-so', he would not mean: '*d* is a so-and-so because I say it is', but: 'I say that *d* is a so-and-so because I think that it is.'

Another objection might be that I have relied too strongly on the notion of 'similarity' as an objective control. Wittgenstein has shown (for example, in the case of 'game') that there is no unitary thread of similarity which runs through the entire class of things which are designated by the same word.[21] Without becoming involved in Wittgensteinian exegesis, I might be permitted to say that I do not believe that my position, especially as it will develop, is at variance with his notion of 'family resemblance'. In the present instance, it is clear that my position certainly does not require that there be an observable, or explicitly statable, similarity between all the members of a class; quite the opposite, for this would amount to the class's being strictly defined. What my position does require is that, as used in a given context, a word have a consistent sense, that there be correct and incorrect uses; incorrect uses being those which are incompatible with, and therefore distort, the sense of the word. 'Game', as we saw, does have such a sense; some things are, and some other things definitely are not, games. Nor does 'game' mean something like 'what people call "games"', because this would not enable us to recognise new games or to acknowledge new legitimate uses of 'game'. To take a striking example, if 'game' had not had an understandable sense, then 'language game' would not have been a powerful explanatory concept; it would merely have represented a decision of Wittgenstein's to use 'game' in a new way.

The disagreement which we have imagined between Jones and Smith is, then, one for which there is hope of a rational settlement. At one point or the other in the course of this investigation, we substituted 'unemployed', 'rifle' and 'deserter' for 'so-and-so', which marked a logical space to be filled by an open-textured word. None of the argument would have had to be changed if we had substituted, say, 'tree', 'cat' or 'man'. Nor would we have had to make any special adjustments if we had substituted 'murder', 'duties of a father', 'sacrilege' or 'lie'. If, as I have been arguing, moral problems are typically questions about the correct application of moral terms (that is to say, whether a course of action is of a given moral type), then these questions can be decided. The interpersonal claim which is a logical feature of moral judgements is a claim which can be tested and established by rational methods.

To say that moral terms can be freely substituted into a formal frame of argument designed to test consistency in the use of open-textured terms is not to deny the distinctiveness of moral discourse. It is simply to say that moral terms are like other open-textured terms in as much as they are open-textured. However, what is being denied is that moral concepts are marked off from other types because they suffer some special logical disability. Moral discourse is distinctive for the same reason that other realms of discourse are distinctive, which is that experience is classified and interpreted from a distinctive point of view. What is interesting about the above argument is not, I think, that I tried, as it were, to slip moral concepts into respectable company through the back door, but that I started with what is generally taken to be a special problem in moral philosophy (the problem, that is, which exercised Lucas) and showed that it is, in fact, a problem in general philosophy.

24. *Open-Texture and the Explication of Concepts*

We can expand the foregoing schema by a closer inspection of open-texture and by a consideration of how open-textured terms are brought to bear upon experience.

I shall start by borrowing heavily from Kovesi's excellent analysis of the concept, 'table'. He notes that, although tables are perceivable objects, there is no perceivable quality of *being-a-table*. What makes an object a table is not that it has certain observable properties but that it satisfies certain physiological and sociological needs: 'Historically, without a need for tables we would not have these pieces of furniture; logically, we cannot understand the notion of a table without understanding that need.' [22] Since the *rationale* of 'table' is shaped by the functions of tables in a way of life, and since such social forms are subject to change, the concept of a table is not, once and for all, determined: 'With changes in our needs and social conventions our reasons for having tables might also change and consequently what will count as a table, and what will not, will also change.' [23] He cites as an example the difference between the ancient Roman and the present-day notions of 'table'. Even more: Kovesi borrows an example from Austin in order to show that the fact that tables have become commercially manufactured objects has further modified the concept 'table':

> We do not only use tables, we also use the word 'table'. And because we do not only want to write or eat on tables but want to sell them or identify them and list them on inventories, the life and use of the word 'table' is shaped by all the various activities; that is, the life and use of the word 'table' is shaped not only by the way we use the object table, but also by all those other activities in the performance of which we have to use the word 'table'.[24]

We have here a good example of how the need for a word to meet the demands of a way of life contributes to the indeterminacy of the *rationale* governing the use of that word. This is one of the prime sources of open-texture; but let us now see how this open-texture manifests itself in the use of the word.

Tables are physical objects with observable properties, but

there is no observable property of being-a-table, nor are the multifarious needs and purposes for which we have tables either physical objects or observable properties. How is the transition made between the *rationale* of 'table' and the observable properties of tables? Clearly the former establishes standards which must be met by the latter. To quote Kovesi again:

> Certain qualities must be present in a piece of furniture in order that we should be able to call it a 'table', but there is no strict rule as to what these qualities must be. There are various ways of making tables, and we can use various materials. On the other hand, not just anything will qualify as a table. Our reasons for having tables constitute, as it were, the guiding principle for deciding what are tables and what are not, or what new constructions will be acceptable as tables.[25]

That there is no strict rule as to the observable properties that an object must have in order to be a table is, Kovesi points out, the reason for saying that 'table' has open-texture. He makes the important distinction (which is too frequently confused) between open-texture as a logical feature of words like 'table' (words, that is, which depend upon the presence of properties *other than that designated by the word itself* for their correct application) and the 'shading' which blurs the distinction between colours: 'Colours can shade into other colours, but this is not the same as having an open texture in the sense in which I want to say that the concept of table has an open texture. The concept of a table has an open texture not because tables can shade into other pieces of furniture but because even the unmistakable tables can be made in a variety of ways and manners.'[26] 'Table' is different from colour-words because it requires the presence of other properties than 'tableness' for its correct application. As the last quoted sentence indicates, it is different from geometry words (e. g., 'rectangle') because tables can be made in a variety of ways; there is no strict rule, as there is with 'rectangle', which prescribes the properties of a table. There is a logical 'gap' between a statement of observable properties and the statement 'This is a table', whereas there is an entailment relationship between a statement about angle-measurements and the statement 'This is a rectangle'.[27]

Let us develop some of the themes introduced by Kovesi in order to fit them into our present discussion. The use of the word 'table' is guided by a *rationale* which is dictated by the roles that tables and the word 'table' play in a way of life. This *rationale* is the standard for the skilful use of 'table'. We can imagine, for example, that a child might use 'table' to refer to all pieces of furniture (which is already better than using it of non-utilitarian objects). He has not yet grasped the *rationale*; he has not got the point of the word 'table'. Also, this *rationale* sets the standard that objects must meet if they are to qualify as tables. However, there is this 'gap' between unobservable purposes and observable objects, between the concept as a *rationale* and the objects which the concept classifies. It would be correct to reply that this gap is crossed by the skill of the knower or speaker and that a skill is a radically inarticulate knowhow. It would be correct, but unhelpful, because the gap is crossed; people do identify objects as tables with remarkably widespread agreement. Upon being challenged, one could offer reasons to support the assertion that this object is a table. There are more ways to cross the gap created by the lack of a strict entailment relationship than by taking a blind leap, whether of faith or of decision. That the process cannot be completely analysed does not mean that it is completely unanalysable.

We can set the gap out starkly by imaging a computer which was programmed with a definition of 'table' which stated the purposes and functions of tables, and no more. Then let us suppose that data were fed into the computer which were collected from various physical objects. These data would represent a complete physico-chemical topography of each object, stating the object's measurements, colour, chemical composition, etc. It is clear that the computer would not be able to register the difference between the sets of data which had been collected from tables and those from other objects. There is, with the given information, no way to find a relationship between the teleological definition and the quantitative data. Yet there is a relationship which we detect consistently in our daily lives. The key to bridging the gap is that the concept is the standard for the object. *If* an object is to qualify as a table, *then* it must meet such-and-such requirements. This information establishes the relationship between the observable features of some objects and the *rationale* of 'table'. Needless to say, it is not my purpose to inquire as to whether, or to what extent, this process can be computerised.

The process by which a content is given to the concept 'table' can be characterised as follows: In order to qualify as tables, objects must be constructed in such a way as to allow people to use them for certain purposes; e. g., to place cups and plates on them, to write on them, etc. Therefore they must be made of suitable material and be suitably designed. But what kind of material? What size and shape must they be? Well, some relatively inflexible material, like wood, stone or metal. As far as design is concerned, they must have flat surfaces, be of a convenient height and size to enable people to use them, etc. The surface of a table can be of almost any shape, depending on what it is to be used for; e. g., a square table for playing bridge, a round table for showing the equality of knights. But not every shape will do; a table could not be a rectangle ten feet long and one-eighth of an inch wide. And so we could go on.

Let us call this process by which we specify the physical requirements of tables the 'explication' of the concept 'table'. The explication is a progressive endeavour, going from vague, general terms (e. g., 'relatively inflexible material') to more specific stages (e. g., 'wood', 'stone', etc.). It is a process which is analogous to the confirmation of a scientific theory in that one can more strictly state what would disqualify an object from being a table (falsification) than one can state the qualifications that an object must meet in order to be a table (verification). If any given table can be described as an object made up of certain observable properties, not all of which (for example, its colour) are relevant to its being a table, then a complete explication of the concept 'table' would be an exhaustive list of all the possible combinations of features, such that the presence of any one of these combinations in an object would justify calling that object a table. There are some clear reasons for saying that such a list could not be compiled. For one thing, one is faced with the notion, associated with logical atomism, of there being one complete and correct description of an object: a notion which Wittgenstein not only repudiated but refuted. Also, there is no limit to the number of possible materials that might be invented, or designs that might be imagined, or uses that might be devised, all of which would have to be incorporated in our proposed explication of 'table'. 'Table' is, thus, an open-textured term.

In general, we can say that a term has open-texture if the explication of its *rationale* is, like the verification of a scientific hypothesis, an essentially incompletable project. In other words, a term is open-textured if the set of the combinations of features which must be present to justify the use of the term is an open set. One could not, that is, make an exhaustive disjunction of all the possible combinations of features, the statement of which could be coupled with a statement about the features of a particular object to entail a conclusion of the form, 'This is an X.'

25. *The Open-Texture of Moral Terms*

One characteristic of ethical behaviour is that it is regulated by rules of conduct: e. g., 'Thou shalt not steal', and 'One ought to keep one's promises'. These rules bear an obvious resemblance to the rules of conduct set out in law. In *The Concept of Law* H. L. A. Hart discusses the open-texture of the latter type of rule. He shows that it enters at two levels. In the first place, any such rule must be phrased in words, some of which, if the rule is to have any content, must be general terms which designate classes of person or thing, types of behaviour, and the like. These terms will be open-textured. There will always be the possibility of cases arising where the applicability of these words, and therefore of the rule, will be in question. Hart says, *à propos* such a case: 'Here something in the nature of a crisis in communication is precipitated; there are reasons both for and against our use of a general term, and no firm convention or general agreement dictates its use, or, on the other hand, its rejection by the person concerned to classify.' [28] (One might note the obvious, but important, point here that there is a problem only because the meaning of the general term and the features of the questionable case are such that it is reasonable to suspect that the case might be subsumed.

Hart uses the example of a rule forbidding vehicles in a park and wonders whether it would apply to a toy motor car. There is no need to wonder whether it would apply to a briefcase one might be carrying or a pipe one might be smoking. Even at this simple level, problems arise only when there is a reason to wonder about something, and one could not understand the problem unless one knew why there was thought to be a problem.)

There is a second level at which rules are open-textured. It does not obviate the first because any rule framed in language (and this is, after all, the most precise way to frame them) will contain words which are open-textured. However, rules can be stated with more or less precision. For example, it would be easy to make provision, one way or the other, for toy motor cars in the rules about vehicles (although one might still face questions about what counted as a toy motor car). Any clarification which is made after the fact could conceivably have been made before the fact and, therefore, all need for interpretation could conceivably have been avoided. Hart says that the reason we cannot frame laws so strictly is that 'we are men, not gods'. (It is perhaps instructive to recall that within the Judaeo-Christian tradition the rules of conduct that have claimed divine legislation have provoked some thirty centuries of casuistry.) He explains why this is so:

> It is a feature of the human predicament (and so of the legislative one) that we labour under two connected handicaps whenever we seek to regulate, unambiguously and in advance, some sphere of conduct by means of general standards to be used without further official directions on particular occasions. The first handicap is our relative ignorance of fact; the second is our relative indeterminacy of aim. If the world in which we live were characterized only by a finite number of features, and these together with all the modes in which they could combine were known to us, then provision could be made in advance for every possibility.[29]

He points out that the indeterminacy of aim is a function of the ignorance;[30] one cannot decide what one does not know. The relatively vague intention of preserving a park for quiet recreation, which motivated the rule against vehicles, must be clarified when the problem of the toy motor cars is confronted; it must be decided 'whether some degree of peace in the park is to be sacrificed to, or defended against, those children whose pleasure or interest is to use these things'.[31]

Hart explains the settlement of these problems of open-texture as a matter of 'choice',[32] and indeed it is. However, it is important to be clear about where choice does enter into the solution both to understand its positive significance and to preclude the illegitimate extension of Hart's argument to questions in moral philosophy. First of all, it is not, as I have pointed out, a matter of choice that one thing (e. g., a toy motor car) presents a problem and something else (e. g., a briefcase or pipe) does not. Secondly, the choice that is made is only indirectly a decision about how a word is to be used. The decision is made at a different level, and because of this decision the correct use of the word in the relevant context is determined. In Hart's example, the choice that is made is not about whether or not to call a toy motor car a 'vehicle', but about the purposes for which the park is to be used; and it is by the clarification of this intention that the verbal question is settled.

The significance of the relevant decision's being a clarification of intention lies in the fact that the purpose of the park provides the *rationale* of the rule prohibiting vehicles, as the purpose of a table provides the *rationale* of the concept 'table'. The problem of whether or not the rule of conduct applied to the questionable case (that is, the problem posed by the open-texture of the rule) was solved by a clarification of the *rationale* behind the rule.

We can begin to relate Hart's conclusions to the question of the open-texture of moral terms by recalling what was said in the last chapter about bridging the gap between the *rationale* of 'table', which had to do with unobservable purposes and needs, and particular tables, which are observable physical objects. The concept requires explication. Moral concepts, like 'murder', designate types of action which are similar only from the moral point of view. But yet the actions which are classified by moral concepts are actions which take place in the public world; they can be observed and given identical descriptions by people who have different, or no, moral standards with regard to them. For example, people who approve, or disapprove, or are indifferent, will all know precisely what Raskolnikov did to the pawnbroker and her sister after reading Dostoyevski's vivid account. Looked at the other way, moral concepts appear to be especially thin in empirical content. 'You say that Raskolnikov murdered them. But what did he do?' To say that 'murder' means 'unjustifiable homicide' is of no help in distinguishing murders from other homicides. It is similar to saying that a table is an object which is used for such-and-such purposes; it enables us to know that we are looking for physical objects (and not, say, mathematical entities), but it does not inform us about the observable features of these objects. 'Murder' (and similar moral concepts), like 'table', needs explication if we are to be able to identify the actions which it designates and, therefore, to be able to use it in the guidance of our own actions and as a tool of moral criticism.

Because the actions of a type designated by a moral term are similar to one another only from the moral point of view, these types cannot be defined in morally neutral terms. On the other hand, the particular actions can be described in morally neutral terms; indeed, they *must* be so describable if moral concepts are to have any relevance to actual behaviour – one cannot imagine for example, how moral instruction could be given using only moral terms. This is the same logical 'gap' which we encountered in the case of 'table'. We saw in the last section how this concept could be explicated by consideration of the standards which it set for entrance into the appropriate class of objects and inferring from this the sort of properties that the objects must have. This is, we saw, a progressive procedure, going from the more general and vague to the more specific. The standard set by a purpose to be fulfilled is translated into a set of standards about the requirements which must be met by the material, the design, etc. These, in turn, can be further specified; e. g., by stating the kinds of material which are suitably inflexible. The controlling norm of the process remains the *rationale* of 'table'; each step of the explication, if it is a correct step, can be traced back to this *rationale*. Thus, if any question should arise as to whether a

particular object is a table, it must be answered by means of a
further explication of 'table' which clarifies the concept sufficiently to allow a judgement to be made in this particular
case, and the correctness of this explication can be checked by
tracing it back to the *rationale* of 'table'.

With this description of how and why the concept 'table' is
explicated, we are enabled to recognise the process at work in
the case of moral concepts. In fact, we have already observed
the explication of the term 'C-resident' in the imaginary argument described by Lucas. (Sections 20 and 21.) As was mentioned, Lucas did not provide us with any information about
the *rationale* by which the class of people who were obliged to
live within $4\frac{1}{2}$ miles of Carfax was formed, but we can presume
that it had something to do with duties that these people had
to perform. Who are C-residents? How does one bridge the
gap between the notion of people being bound by a residence
requirement and proper names? In the first place, it has to do
with the duties performed by professors; so C-residents are
professors. But not all professors – only those who profess soft-
option subjects. But not all soft-option professors – not those
who perform experiments. And so on. In the first of the two
arguments we observe the progressive explication of the concept 'C-resident'; in the second, each move was defended by
such an explication. We can note in this case the same
characteristic which was found in the explication of 'table';
namely, that one can more strictly state disqualifications than
qualifications. The first step in the explication of 'C-resident'
is that the people who must perform duties which require
them to live within $4\frac{1}{2}$ miles of Carfax are professors. (Other
people might have duties which require them to live close to
the centre of Oxford, but in the context of the imagined argument, the duties in question are clearly duties which are in-
cumbent upon professors *qua* professors.) We know that *only*
professors have these duties, but we do not know that *all*
professors do; we know that *only*, but not *all*, soft-option
professors do, etc. The point is, as we saw with 'table', that the
positive statement of qualifications which is the explication of
a concept is necessary if particular instances of the relevant
class are to be identified, but it is necessarily incompletable.

It would not be difficult to imagine an explication of an

authentic moral concept, like 'murder', which would be along the same lines as that of 'C-resident' and would, therefore, be capable of the same sort of analysis. Suppose that a policeman and a criminal are in conversation

P: You were wrong to murder that bank clerk.
C: What was wrong about it?
P: You killed him, and killing is wrong.
C: How about you? You shot Pete Jones.
P: But that was in self-defence.
C: All right. But what about Sam Smith? They hanged him when he was defenceless and offered no threat to them.
P: But he was a convicted murderer.

The policeman has his notion of what justifies the taking of human life (with which notion we obviously need not agree) and is able to clarify that notion sufficiently to enable him to decide what is, and what is not, 'murder'. An explication of this concept, in accordance with common standards, would show it to include such things as killing in the course of an armed robbery, killing to inherit money, killing because the victim is a Jew or a Negro, and to exclude killing in legitimate self-defence. Since there is widespread disagreement about them, abortion, euthanasia and capital punishment are, by common standards, questionable cases.

I shall return to the question of how the explication of moral concepts is brought to bear on the settling of moral problems. My present purpose is to show how this explication is related to the open-texture of moral terms. The purpose of the explication is to identify empirically describable actions, or types of action, to which the corresponding moral term applies, and which are, therefore, right or wrong. As we have already seen (sections 7 and 8), these empirical descriptions can never exhaustively describe the moral type. Moral terms are open-textured in that their explication is an incompletable process.

If we look now at the form that the explication of moral concepts takes, we see that it is something like this: a type of action which can be described in morally neutral terms (e. g., killing a bank clerk in the course of an armed robbery) is identified as an instance of a moral type (e. g., murder) and, therefore, right or wrong, depending upon the concept which is being explicated. That is to say, the explication of a moral concept takes the form of rules of conduct. Now, we saw that Hart's analysis of rules of conduct shows that these rules themselves have open-texture on two counts: (a) the open-texture of the words in which they are couched; and (b) the impossibility of foreseeing and accounting for every possible combination of circumstances in the framing of these rules. Thus, moral terms have an open-texture on three different counts: the two described by Hart as inherent to rules of conduct and that introduced by the fact that moral concepts cannot be completely explicated into rules of conduct. We could also mention that the explication of moral concepts, proceeding as it does by way of example and by the extension of judgements to similar cases, more closely resembles legal precedent than it does legislation, and Hart has pointed out that the former, because of the lack of specificity, is even more open than the latter.

Hart's analysis also illustrates the way in which questions about the correct application of a rule are settled by a suitable clarification of the *rationale* behind the rule. In his example this amounted to getting a clearer notion about what the park was to be used for. The purposes for which a plot of land was set aside as a park functioned in the same way as did the purposes for which pieces of material were fashioned as tables, as the controlling norm to which all particular questions are ultimately referred. This same is true of moral concepts. If we take 'murder' as an example again, we have already seen that the 'kernel' of its *rationale* is that the taking of human life requires a special justification. If we ask *why* this is so, we get a statement of the *rationale*; if we ask *what follows* from this, we get an explication of that *rationale*. When we are not sure what follows from the *rationale* of 'murder' – that is, when there is perplexity about whether or not a particular act or type of homicide is justified – we must go back again to the first question: why does the taking of human life require a special justification?, and try to get a clearer answer than we had before. Obviously, this explicit procedure is not generally followed in the making of moral judgements, any more than it is followed when judgements are given on the basis of legal precedent. The point is that there is an implicit *rationale* behind a precedent (moral or legal) which is followed in assimilating a new case to the precedent and which must be clarified if this assimilation is challenged.

The big difference between Hart's example and the example of 'murder' is that the *rationale* behind his rule followed from the intention of the legislator whereas that of 'murder' has no such source. That the taking of human life requires special justification cannot be said to be a matter of choice in the same sense that the decision to set aside a park for certain purposes can be said to be a matter of choice. The *rationale* of a person's concept of murder has its roots deep within that person's set of beliefs about the world and about the meaning of human life, and not within some relatively specific intention framed within a limited practical context. One of the chief factors contributing to open-texture is that concepts are interrelated within a system of concepts and that any modification of the system (by the introduction of new concepts or by changing the old) brings about a modification of the concepts themselves; concepts are not like the individual stones in a pile which remain unchanged except in their external relations when the pile is disturbed – a change in the conceptual scheme always entails a modification of the existing concepts. We see the importance of this in the case of 'murder', whose *rationale* is, so to speak, at the mercy of an indefinitely wide range of other concepts, any shifting of which will cause reverberations in the concept of murder. One can see a striking example of this by considering what the giving up of Christianity, or the taking up of Marxism, can do to a person's notion of the value of human life and, consequently, to his concept of murder.

Moral terms, then, are open-textured for (at least) the following reasons: (a) as is the case with words generally, the *rationale* which governs the use of a moral term is indeterminate; (b) this *rationale* is sensitive to conceptual modifications over an indefinite range of the conceptual scheme, which means that it is itself subject to alteration because of conceptual changes elsewhere; (c) the *rationale* cannot be completely explicated in morally neutral terms; (d) its explication takes the form of moral rules which cannot be framed to meet every possible contingency; (e) these rules are expressed in open-textured terms.

Thus, to say that moral terms are open-textured is not to point to a curious, but unimportant, logical oddity about these terms. Nor is it to say something trivial, like saying that we cannot draw a sharp line between red and orange because these colours shade into one another. It is to say something of the utmost importance about the logical structure of moral concepts. It is to relate these concepts to the general conceptual scheme and to show how they are brought to bear on the interpretation of concrete human behaviour and, *therefore*, on moral decisions. It is to explain the flexibility, evolution, and even the change, of moral rules without the need to retreat into an irrationalism or voluntarism, which can all too easily become the justification (in fact, logically *ought* to become the justification) for the enthronement of power as the source of right. It is, in short, the beginning of an understanding of what moral discourse is.

26.   *Open-Texture and Substantial Moral Problems*

The obvious objection to my project of treating moral problems as problems which arise because of the open-texture of moral terms is that I am trivialising the subject. Such an objection might take one of two forms. (1) It might be claimed that I am reducing ethics to logic; that is, I am confusing substantial moral problems with merely verbal questions. (2) It might be admitted that the method I am proposing is all right as far as it goes, but that it does not go nearly far enough. All it equips one to do is to deal with the relatively unimportant problems that arise at the fringe of currently held concepts. The method ignores the really important issues, the novel situations where we have no rules to guide us. This second objection also implies a charge of moral conservatism, an attempt on my part to keep imposing the old categories where they no longer fit. I shall deal with each of these in turn.

Concerning the charge that I am reducing moral problems to linguistic questions, let me recall what I said in the last section about the ambiguity attached to the notion of 'agreeing on the use of words' and how there is a sense in which we could use that phrase in which the agreement reached would be the result of a serious inquiry and would represent a change of mind as well as of word. Further, let me recall what I said in Part One, that the application of a moral term (like 'murder') is a moral judgement. Therefore, a question about the correct use of a moral term is a moral problem.

The distinction between 'merely verbal' and 'substantial' is one which Hare finds to be of great importance in differentiating 'descriptive' from 'evaluative' language (of which moral language is a sub-class). He claims that at least part of the distinction between the two lies in the fact that, in the case of descriptive language, universalisability is a merely verbal matter, whereas, in the case of evaluative language, it is a substantial question. Let us first see how he explains this and then try to relate it to our present question about the correct use of moral terms.

Hare first establishes the universalisability of descriptive terms using 'red' as a 'typical example of a descriptive term':[33]

> If a person says that a thing is red, he is committed to the view that anything which was like it in the relevant respects would likewise be red. The relevant respects are those which, he thought, entitled him to call the first thing red; in this particular case, they amount to one respect only; its red colour. This follows, according to the definitions given above, from the fact that 'This is red' is a descriptive judgment. 'This is red' entails 'Everything like this in the relevant respects is red' simply because to say that something is red while denying that some other thing which resembles it in the relevant respects is red is to misuse the word 'red'; and this is because 'red' is a descriptive term, and because therefore to say that something is red is to say that it is of a certain kind, and so to imply that anything which is of that same kind is red.[34]

In answering one of the objections which he raises against this thesis, he clarifies his position on our present point:

> It might be said that the universal proposition which is generated, in the way described above, by any singular descriptive judgment is merely a matter of the *meaning* of the

descriptive term contained in the judgment; that it cannot be a matter of substance. If I say that X is red, I am committed to holding that anything which is like X in a certain respect is red too. In using the descriptive term 'red' I must be employing *some* universal rule; but, it might be objected, this rule is only that which gives the meaning of 'red'; it is a purely verbal matter of how the word 'red' is used. Now this I do not wish to deny, in the case of purely descriptive terms; as we shall see, evaluative terms differ in this respect.[35]

Now one would not, of course, want to disagree about the universalisability of descriptive terms for the very reason which Hare puts so succinctly: '. . . to say that something is red is to say that it is of a certain kind, and so to imply that anything which is of that same kind is red'. Nor would one want to deny that a person who calls one thing an X and refuses to call another thing which is like it in the relevant respects an X is guilty of a misuse of the term X. That is to say, one is logically obliged to apply the same descriptive term to different cases which are alike in the relevant respects. But what one *would* like to deny is that one is logically obliged to acknowledge that two things *are* alike in relevant respects. In other words, the *application* of descriptive terms (the recognition that two things are of the same kind, the judgement 'This is an X') is a *substantial, not a logical, inference.*

This is clouded by Hare's choosing 'red' as 'a typical example of a descriptive term'. That it is not typical is evinced by his own explanation: 'The relevant respects are those which, he thought, entitled him to call the first thing red; in this particular case, *they amount to one respect only: its red colour.*' (My italics.) Colour words are, rather, untypical in that there are no mediating conditions required for their application; there are no relevant respects which entitle one to use them other than the presence of the colour itself. Most common descriptive words (e. g., 'table') are not like this.

When I call an object in the dining-room a table, it is because of the presence in that object of certain properties. If I then refuse to call an object in the sitting-room a table, I am not committing a *logical* error, since, I am presuming, this object has different properties from those that the first had. It would be no good to argue that they are similar in the relevant respects and that the factual differences (of construction or shape) are irrelevant. How does one determine which facts are relevant or irrelevant? If I am to be logically obliged to acknowledge that an object is a table, there must be a logical entailment between a statement asserting the presence of certain specified properties and the conclusion 'This is a table', which, as we have already seen, would require a definition of 'table' in terms of observable properties. We have also seen that such a definition cannot be given. One cannot specify exactly what shapes, sizes, materials, etc., tables can be made of, to the exclusion of all others. If some Danish designer comes out with a radically new line of furniture, we do not refuse to acknowledge that some of the pieces are tables even though they are different in every respect from anything that we have seen before; nor are we changing the meaning of 'table' when we recognise new designs as further instances of the same type of thing.

Since the open-texture of terms like 'table' precludes the possibility of defining them in terms of observable properties and, therefore, the possibility of a logical entailment of a judgement like 'This is a table' from a statement about observable properties, the application of these descriptive terms is not a 'merely verbal' matter but a matter of 'substance'. If this is true of 'table', it is certainly true of 'murder' and other moral terms. Because they are moral terms, their application is a moral judgement; because they are open-textured terms, it is a substantial judgement.

I shall treat the second objection from three angles: (a) the notion of the unimportance of the problems raised because of open-texture; (b) the charge of moral conservatism; (c) the question of new, *sui generis*, problems.

Logic does not provide a measure of ethical importance. That the gap between a presently held concept and a problematic case is not wide does not imply that the problem is not important. If a mother were to kill her child to relieve him from a painful and incurable disease, the action is as near as you please to being a murder, but this does not render the decision any the less important. On the contrary, it is precisely its proximity to the recognised moral type that makes it such an important and excruciating decision. The Muslims and the Crusaders did not scruple over killing one another because they did not wonder whether it was murder; they knew it was their duty.

Nor is it true that problems which arise on the fringe of moral concepts are merely isolated instances, like that of the mother, which, though of great personal importance, are not of widespread interest because they are not frequently repeated. Let me show that this is not so in the case of 'murder'. It is clear, first of all, that what is characteristic of murder from the moral point of view is that it is *unjustifiable* homicide. It is because of this factor that 'murder' has the sort of open-texture discussed in the last section; it is the question of what is to count as a sufficient reason for taking a human life which is, we might say, the really important issue when it comes to deciding problems about murder. 'Homicide' is decidedly the junior partner; it is not even a moral term. However, I want to point out that important moral problems arise even because this morally neutral term is open-textured. One can think of at least three serious problems of medical ethics which have to do with questions of what is, and what is not, homicide: (a) Is it a human who was killed? This is of paramount importance in the question of the morality of abortion. It is not the only serious question about abortion, of course, but that it is important can be seen from the fact that people who think that someone would have a duty to have an appendix or a tumour removed think that it is a crime to have a foetus removed and that, on the other hand, people approve of the aborting of a foetus for reasons for which they would never condone infanticide. If, for example, Aquinas's theory, based on the notion of the 'eduction of forms', that the rational soul is not infused (and, therefore, a human person produced) until the matter is properly disposed to receive that form (approximately the stage of viability) were able to be established as true, the problem of abortion would be substantially altered. (b) Did the action in question cause the death? This has obvious relevance to questions about due care and diligence and to questions about the removal of life-prolonging equipment. (c) Did the action (which was certainly sufficient to cause death – e. g., the cutting out of the heart) cause death, or was the person dead already? That is: When is someone dead or alive? This problem has been given a good deal of publicity recently because of the development of transplantation techniques.

Thus, questions which arise on the fringe of the concept of murder, and on the least important fringe at that, give rise to substantial problems of widespread importance. Ethical interest and importance are not functions of the breadth of the logical gap between the *rationale* of a moral term and the features of a questionable case.

The answer to the question about the importance of problems raised because of the open-texture of moral terms leads into the question of moral conservatism. To say that abortion is a problem about the extension of the concept 'murder' is not to pre-judge the issue, but to locate it. It is to say that abortion raises (at least) these two questions: (a) Is the termination of a pregnancy the killing of a human person? (b) If it is, can it be justified, perhaps by analogy with self-defence? Moreover, to come to a conclusion about the morality of abortion, or euthanasia, or capital punishment – all of which are problems about the extension of 'murder' – is to make an important advance in moral thinking; it is to establish (perhaps to change) moral standards concerning a large and important class of human actions. It is to shape a new moral concept which will itself be subject to the vicissitudes of open-texture. This concept will be either a subclass (and, therefore, a specification) of the concept 'murder' or will be distinguished from 'murder' as a type of justifiable homicide, like self-defence.

There is some value in the suggestion that we should take a fresh approach to moral problems and not try to fit them into the old categories, so long as we understand what this means. It certainly cannot mean that, for example, with abortion we should not question whether, on either count, it is unjustifiable homicide, that we should treat it on its own grounds without worrying about whether a foetus is a human person and without considering the possibility of drawing analogies with the reasons which, in other instances, are thought to justify homicide. Such a suggestion simply does not make sense. If we did not worry about whether a foetus was a human, we would not worry about abortion; it would be just another surgical operation. If we did not think that there might be reasons which justify the killing of a foetus which would not justify the killing of an infant, we would not wonder whether abortion was wrong – we would know it was. There would be no point in gathering factual data about the human foetus, in considering the consequences of terminating pregnancies, in making excruciating, and universalisable, moral decisions – indeed we would have no idea about what facts to investigate, which consequences to consider; we would have no notion that a moral decision was required or that we ought to institute an inquiry – unless we knew that abortion was a moral problem and why it was a moral problem.

It is not moral conservatism to say that moral problems arise when people are perplexed about the precise extent of their moral concepts. Moral conservatism is the belief that moral concepts have been, once and for all, adequately explicated and that the rules of conduct thereby expressed represent the final moral truth. To say that moral terms are open-textured is to destroy the grounds of moral conservatism, for it is to say that the *rationale* of a moral term (which is itself indeterminate, being shaped within a way of life, being dependent upon a great many other beliefs about matters affecting the human condition, being ever susceptible to a deeper understanding and a more articulate expression) cannot be completely and finally explicated and that even a given explication is in the form of open-textured rules. To say this is not to deny that there is such a thing as moral truth; it is to say that, if moral truth is to be found, it is to be found primarily in the *rationale* and that any given explication of that *rationale* can make only a secondary, and derived, claim to be true, which claim can be invalidated, not only by developments that might take place at the level of the *rationale*, but also by changes in historical circumstances. For example, the belief that homicide requires a special justification makes a claim to be true (or, if you will, 'valid' or 'rationally justified') that can not be made by rules which, at one time or another, are formulated about war, capital punishment, abortion, etc. The invention of thermo-nuclear and biological weaponry can bring about a reconsideration of the rules about a 'just war' without requiring a deepening of understanding or a change of belief about the value of human life. A good example of how an argument which relies implicitly on the open-texture of moral terms can oppose moral conservatism is provided by the recent controversy within the Catholic Church about the morality of birth control. Both the defenders of the *status quo* and the proponents of change claimed to be basing their arguments on the significance of sex-in-marriage. The conservatives argued that a belief in moral truth (and, of course, the belief that the Church has unfailingly taught such truth) requires that the rule forbidding birth control remain unchanged. One of the more powerful arguments of the progressives was that a deeper understanding of the role of sex in the married life has revealed that it has functions other than, and at least as important as, that of procreating children, and, therefore, the rule should be modified. In other words, the conservatives said that the concept had been explicated once and for all; the progressives claimed that a clarification of the *rationale* necessitated a further explication.

It is not only the moral conservatives who think that the critical point in moral truth is to be found in the explication of moral concepts. Many proponents of radical theories in moral philosophy make the same mistake. A good deal of the controversy that has raged about the questions of absolutism *versus* relativism, objectivism *versus* subjectivism, about naturalism, cognitivism, etc., has centred on the logical status of the rules of conduct which are the explication of moral concepts. The truth of a moral belief depends upon the truth of a great many other beliefs, and even then there are questions about its right to be called 'true'; but one thing that the question does *not* depend upon is the capacity of a moral concept to be explicated into a set of exceptionless, universally and eternally valid, rules, any more than the intelligibility of 'table' depends upon an exhaustive list of the observable properties that tables might possess.

We come now to the question of novel, *sui generis*, moral problems. Do moral problems ever arise which have no bearing upon our previous moral beliefs and in the solution of which, therefore, our accepted moral concepts have no relevance? It would be impossible to prove that this could not happen, but I have never heard of such a problem and I think that there are good reasons for thinking that it could not arise. It is certainly true that the cases sometimes put forward by philosophers as requiring decisions where there are no rules to guide us are not this sort of problem. As examples we can take Sartre's famous dilemma, alluded to earlier, about the young man who was torn between staying home to care for his mother and going off to join the Free French Army, and a case proposed by Hare about two tax-experts, both completely conversant with the facts, who cannot agree on the morality of a particular attempt at tax avoidance. Neither of these is a *sui generis* problem in the sense which we gave that term at the beginning of this paragraph. A young man from a different society (say a young Spartan) in which family ties were not so highly valued would not have been confronted with a moral problem. Nor, in the second instance, would a man have a problem who did not believe that he had a moral obligation to pay taxes or who thought, even, that it would be wrong to pay taxes to support what he considered to be an immoral government. I am not saying that people do not bear the burden of responsibility in making moral decisions; I am saying that people are faced with moral decisions because of their moral beliefs and that without such beliefs there would be no occasions which called for moral decisions. Nor am I denying that there can be situations which are *sui generis* in the sense that they are constituted by a unique set of circumstances. What I am saying is that a moral problem arises when, in the welter of factual circumstance, the agent suspects that he detects a pattern in which some of these facts stand out as relevant and significant. Facts, as we have seen, are relevant only in relation to a moral concept.

William James has said: 'We feel neither curiosity nor wonder concerning things so far beyond us that we have no concepts to refer them to or standards by which to measure them.'[36] This seems to be certainly true of moral problems. If someone claims to have a moral problem about something which bears no relation to our moral concepts (for example, about whether to buy a new car or whether to take a walk by the sea) we are perplexed, not about whether the course of action is right or wrong, but about why he thinks that there is a problem. People with a highly developed gift of moral insight can see moral problems where the rest of us cannot. But if they want to bring the problem home to us, they do not keep repeating the problem or describing the relevant facts; they give us reasons for thinking that there is a problem; that is, they relate it to our moral concepts. There does not seem to be any reason to deny that moral problems arise, as a general rule, in relation to presently held moral beliefs which are incorporated in moral concepts.

Since we are discussing *problems*, we are concerned with cases in which one is perplexed about what is right; which is to say, one is not sure what one's moral belief is in this particular case. It does happen, and perhaps frequently, that a problem of correct classification arises simply because of factual ignorance: '*If* such-and-such is true, *then* this is a case of so-and-so and therefore right (or wrong).' Such a problem can be solved simply by getting the facts straight, which process is conducted, of course, under the guidance of the relevant moral concept. The more interesting type of problem is that in which there is not a doubt of fact, but a doubt about what the facts amount to, when there are good reasons for thinking that the case in question is of a type about which one is morally committed, but also good reasons for thinking that it is not, when the questionable case is similar in many respects to the plain case, but different from it also in some important respects. Such is a problem which is posed by the open-texture of moral terms. To stress this conceptual, or linguistic, aspect is not to trivialise moral problems, nor is it to condone moral conservatism. It is not even the case that the concept under whose banner the moral inquiry is carried out remains sacrosanct. A problem could well inaugurate an inquiry which would lead one not only to clarify, but to question the *rationale* because of which the problem arose. If such were the case, the questioning would of necessity be conducted from the point of view of other concepts; otherwise, it would be in the nature of a *sui generis* problem, and we would not be able to understand that it was, or why it was, a problem. The structure of the problem would not have changed; only the terms of reference.

27.   *Deciding Moral Issues*

We have seen that questions about the correct application of open-texture terms are, in principle, decidable. Let us now see how the method works with moral problems. If we tie together the various threads of argument that have gone before, we shall see that they demonstrate that moral problems are susceptible of a solution which claims interpersonal validity; that is to say, that moral inquiry satisfies the criterion of objectivity that there be a method of settling issues by means of which anybody, in principle, can be brought to agree about what is right or wrong.

Briefly, we have seen that the ability to judge consistently in moral matters (which ability we assumed as given) implies the ability to recognise a similarity between actions from a distinctive, moral point of view. A moral judgement which meets the demands of logical consistency is the judgement that the action under consideration is (or is not) similar, from the moral point of view, to other actions about which an opinion (an agreed opinion when more than one person is concerned in the inquiry) had already been reached; that is, it is assimilated to (or discriminated from) a type of action designated by a moral term (where we have terms to express our moral concepts). Moral terms are open-textured; which means, in part, that they cannot be completely and finally explicated into rules of conduct which are expressed in terms of morally neutral types of action (although such explication is necessary if our moral concepts are to 'come to grips' with actual situations). Moral problems, when they are not questions of fact, are questions about the applicability of moral terms; they arise, that is to say, because of the open-texture of moral terms. Questions about the correct application of open-textured terms are decidable because: (a) there is an objective control to the inquiry; viz., the established 'sense' of the word, which is independent of the activity of the inquirers both because it is a public fact of language and because it is a function of the similarity between the agreed instances, and similarity cannot be decided by *fiat*; and (b) there is a method by which this 'sense' can be brought to bear on the questionable instance; viz., the method of conceptual clarification proposed by Lucas.

Thus, moral problems are, in principle, soluble. In order to see how this would work in practice, let us recall the structure of a moral concept. The 'sense' of a moral term is the *rationale* which underlies its use. This is brought into contact with concrete situations by means of the process of explication by which rules of conduct are generated which specify various types of action in morally neutral terms. This is analogous to the explication of 'table' by which it is inferred what sort of observable properties an object must have in order to meet the requirements set out in the *rationale*. The purpose of the explication of moral terms is to determine what types of action (or of person or situation, since these are frequently relevant to judgements about the right action), described in morally neutral terms, meet the requirements set out in the *rationale*. We can consider a moral concept as encompassing both the *rationale* and its explication.

There are, then, four basic types of moral problem: (I) When neither the *rationale* nor its explication is in question, but there is doubt as to whether the questionable case meets the specification. This is a question of fact. (II) There is doubt about whether the relevant word in the explication ought to apply to the case in question. This requires a clarification of the sense in which the word is used in that context, which is performed in the light of the underlying *rationale*; that is to say the solution of the problem requires that there be a further explication of the concept. (III) The correctness of the explication is in doubt. This requires a reconsideration of the *rationale* and, if need be, a new explication. (IV) The *rationale* itself is in question. This requires an investigation into its basis, which shifts the grounds of the inquiry by changing the terms of reference.

I shall now illustrate these types of problem, and show the logic of their solution in four model arguments. I shall use as my example the argument imagined by Lucas about who is a 'C-resident' because even though this artificial problem exhibits all the logical features of a full-blown moral problem, it can be treated, and the features exhibited, without forcing a choice between the unacceptable alternatives of introducing suitable complexity (and thus obscuring the logical pattern) or of over-simplifying (and thus risking that the method appear ludicrous because of the distortion of the moral reality).

We noted before that the argument between the Professor of Ethiopian Language and Culture (*E*) and the Professor of Comparative Education (*C*) depended upon the facts that *E* believes that there is a class of people who are obliged to live within $4\frac{1}{2}$ miles of Carfax and that *C* both knows that *E* has this belief and understands the *rationale* (at least to some extent) by which the members of this class are identified. There are several positions that *C* might take *vis-à-vis* this belief of *E*'s: (a) He might be in complete agreement, but wonder whether a particular person is a C-resident because of a factual question. (Problem-type I.) (b) He might be in general agreement (and be conversant with the facts) but want to question whether the term ought to apply in a given case. (Problem-type II.) (c) He might agree in principle, but think that *E* has missed the point of 'C-resident'. (Problem-type III.) (d) He might doubt that there is such a class of people. (Problem-type IV.) (We can disregard, for our purposes, the very likely alternative: that *C* does not believe that anyone is a C-resident, but grants it for the sake of argument, perhaps because this is the sort of intellectual game that professors are supposed to engage in over port.) Depending upon what *C* thinks about C-residents, the argument might take one of the following forms:

Argument I:
   C: You said that I ought to live within $4\frac{1}{2}$ miles of Carfax because I profess a 'soft-option' subject. Well, what about the Professor of Experimental Theology?
   E: Ah, but he conducts experiments.
   C: So he does, I had forgotten about that.

Argument II :
   C: You said that I ought to live within $4\frac{1}{2}$ miles of Carfax because I profess a 'soft-option' subject. Well, what about the Professor of Experimental Theology?
   E: Ah, but he conducts experiments.

C: You're right; that makes a difference. But what about the Professor of Natural Philosophy? He hasn't conducted experiments in years.

E: Yes, but his chair is historically an experimental one.

C: Just a moment! I'm willing to agree that the ordinary professors should live in town and that the experimental professors need not, but I cannot go along with the absurd suggestion that some can claim the privileges of the experimenters merely because their predecessors in the dim and distant past conducted experiments.

E: I think that you are missing the point. It's not as if it were an inherited privilege. But let me ask you: why do you think that experimental professors should be exempt?

C: Why, let me see . . . I suppose it's because their responsibilities are different from the rest of us. They fulfil their duties so long as they are on hand to supervise experiments; when their labs are inactive, their presence is not required. They don't have to be available to every don or distressed undergraduate who wants to discuss some problem with them.

E: Precisely! Now the same thing is true, *mutatis mutandis*, of those holding chairs which are traditionally experimental. Their only responsibilities are to the research students under their supervision, and this can surely be taken care of by scheduling appointments.

C: Let me get this clear. You are saying, I think, that the Professor of Natural Philosophy is exempt from the residence requirement since, because of the original purpose of his position, his responsibilities more closely resemble those of the experimental professors than those of what we might call the departmental professors.

E: That is absolutely correct.

C: Then that would mean, I take it, that the same thing would apply to any professor whose duties were confined to research supervision, as, for instance, our friend the Professor of Transfinite and Imaginary Calculus.

E: I had never thought of him in this respect, but now that you mention it, I should certainly have to agree with you.

Argument III:

E: You ought to live within $4\frac{1}{2}$ miles of Carfax.

C: Don't tell me that you subscribe to the ridiculous notion that some professors are bound by such a requirement.

E: Of course I do. Don't you?

C: My calling it 'ridiculous' should indicate what I think.
I don't see any sense to it at all.

E: Well, it certainly makes sense to me. After all, it is the
duty of a professor, unless he is concerned only with research,
to be near at hand so that he can be approached by anyone
under his jurisdiction who has a problem.

C: I think I see what you are getting at, and I would want
to agree with what I take to be the underlying reason, but I do
not agree with your interpretation of it. You are equating being 'readily available for consultation' with being 'near at
hand'. But with the advent of the telephone and the motor car
one can fulfil the first condition without necessarily fulfilling
the second.

E: Yes, you are right. I suppose that I haven't sufficiently
re-examined my beliefs in the light of changed circumstances.

Argument IV: (which starts in the middle of III)

E: Well, it certainly makes sense to me. After all, it is the
duty of a professor, unless he is concerned only with research,
to be near at hand so that he can be approached by anyone
under his jurisdiction who has a problem.

C: Nonsense! The notion that professors have to be
available to all and sundry is a pernicious myth.

E: Of course, experimental professors needn't.

C: I do not accept that distinction. No professors have
duties along those lines *qua* professors, although they might in
their roles as members of a college or of a faculty committee.

E: That is an interesting suggestion. Just how do you con-
ceive of the duties of a professor? . . .

In each of the first three arguments, the disagreement was
resolved. The method by which it was resolved depended
upon the nature of the problem, which was determined by the
extent of previous agreement between *C* and *E*: (I) factual
clarification; (II) further explication of the concept; (III)
re-explication of the concept. In *Argument* IV the disagreement
was more profound in that *C* challenged the *rationale* of
'C-resident'. This required a shift in the focus of the inquiry.

The *rationale* of 'C-resident' ceased to function as the point of reference and became, instead, the subject of the inquiry. This change in focus necessitated the finding of another reference-point, which was clearly suggested by the context: the concept 'duties of a professor'. The *rationale* of this concept (which is shaped by the existing practice of the university, including such factors as precedent and statute) now provides the context of the inquiry, and it is clear that the disagreement between the two professors might be in the form of any one of the four problem-types. If it is one of the first three types, settlement may be reached by the appropriate method of argument, as above. From this point of agreement, they can work out an agreeable conclusion concerning 'C-resident'. If their disagreement is of the fourth type, then it is clear that they will have to move again, and perhaps again, until they find something relevant to the problem that they agree about. The disagreement could be quite profound; perhaps *C* does not believe that anyone has 'duties' or perhaps he disapproves of the institution of 'professorship' (while surreptitiously keeping the title) as deriving from an obsolete authoritarian conception of the university. The point is, that it would be useless for *E* to keep providing distinctions and sub-distinctions of the concept 'C-resident' if his colleague did not believe, for one reason or another, that there was such a thing, or even if there were a conceptual difference between them such as would be manifested in problem-type III. If there is to be any hope for rational argumentation, it is necessary that the problem be located (i. e., the area of disagreement be identified) and this requires that a point of agreement be found. Without this amount of clarification, the discussion cannot be fruitfully, or sensibly, continued. When the point of agreement has been established, there is no reason, in principle, why agreement could not be reached about the original problem. You might ask: But what if they do not agree about anything? A short, but correct, answer would be: If they can talk together, they must have *something* in common.

The big difficulty to be overcome in making the transition from 'C-resident' to actual moral concepts is in trying to accommodate the overwhelming complexity to be found in authentic moral problems. Since the *rationale* of the moral concept is the keystone of moral inquiry, we can start there. There is very little choice in possible answers to the question: Why is anybody obliged to live within $4\frac{1}{2}$ miles of Carfax? However, there is hardly any limit to the number of answers that might be given to the question: Why does the taking of human life require a special justification? And the answers that are given will not be relatively simple ones, like saying that professors have certain duties that require them to be readily available to members of their departments. Even if one could give a straightforward answer to the question about 'murder', the terms in which it was framed would embody an infinity of presuppositions, any of which might conceivably be called into question. Add to this the fact that this *rationale* is seldom articulated to any great extent, but is implicit in the use of 'murder'. Then, one must consider the explication of this *rationale*; that is, in the light of the reasons for saying that homicide requires a special justification, one must consider what sort of reasons would, and would not, meet the standards. One must think of common reasons, such as war,* capital punishment, vengeance, self-defence, etc. But one must at least lay the groundwork for dealing with relatively rare and unforeseeable cases. It is here that the problem of open-texture becomes especially acute and that there is particular need for clarification of the *rationale*, for what is required is that one relate one's reasons for valuing human life to whatever compelling reason is proposed as a justification for taking human life.

The complexity is multiplied, as we see from the last consideration, by the fact that moral concepts do not operate in a vacuum. This, too, follows at least partly from the open-texture of moral terms. Because moral types do not have clear-cut lines of demarcation, questionable cases arise. Sometimes these are doubts about only one moral type; for example, if one wants to do something for some morally neutral reason, but wonders if it might be morally wrong to do it – say one wants to make some money in a business deal, but wonders if it might be dishonest. Sometimes, though, it is more difficult, because the questionable case is also potentially an instance of

*And not only for 'war', but also for a particular war, and for a particular act of war.

another moral type which would require a different response. This is the stuff that moral dilemmas are made of. The problem that faces one when a situation is a potential member of incompatible types is basically one of correct classification. (If this seems a rather pallid explanation of the existential anguish of someone confronted with a dilemma, may I add that I am referring to the problem in as much as it is a problem of *understanding*.) One feels the disorientation that is common when confronted with the apparently random. (A good example is provided by experiences in which one can not attain visual focus; one loses 'control' of the situation.)

The possibility of a solution of anomalous cases lies in the fact that concepts not only do not operate in a vacuum, but that they are not discrete components of the conceptual scheme. Each concept has its rational 'roots' deep within the conceptual system, and has complex relations with an indefinite number of other concepts. Thus, it is possible to bring the conflicting concepts into relation with one another. What is required is that one find a point of view from which the problem can be put into perspective. There is no denying that this is not a painless task, but it is something that has been done many times, and therefore can be done again. All our moral concepts are examples of the attainment of such a point of view. That we can distinguish 'murder' from 'homicide', for example, is the result of the solution of conflicts such as those under discussion. We can make this distinction because we have decided that, in certain conflicts of value when the taking of human life is involved, killing is justified, and that in certain others it is not. If we did not have the concept 'murder', every case which involved homicide would be a moral dilemma because we would have no idea how to tell what reasons do, and what reasons do not, justify homicide. Every moral problem is a conflict of some sort. As our moral concepts develop we become adept at identifying the types of more and more cases. But there will always be more.

To say that moral problems are complex, and that the solution of some of them would seem to require infinite time, patience and wisdom is not to say that moral problems are, in principle, insoluble. Regardless of the complexity of the factors that enter into the construction of a moral concept, they have the structure that we have been discussing, and when problems arise, they will, I think, be of one of the four types which I have identified. One of the great difficulties caused by the complexity of moral concepts is that the problem-type of a given moral problem is not always apparent. As a result, people frequently fail to locate the problem and argue at cross purposes. A common failure, as I have mentioned, is to concentrate too much attention on the explication of a concept rather than where it belongs, on the *rationale*.

Moral problems are decidable, I have been arguing, so long as the disputants can agree upon the *rationale* of the relevant moral concept. It is not that they need to reach agreement *in toto* about the *rationale*, but, as Lucas demonstrated, that they must be able to clarify it sufficiently to enable them to reach agreement about the correct classification of the questionable case.

But can the necessary point of prior agreement always be found? Can it not be the case, perhaps even frequently, that conceptual differences are such that there is no common ground? As was the case with the question of the possibility of *sui generis* moral problems, one hesitates to be dogmatic about this. However, there seem to be good reasons for saying that this cannot be the case. As Wittgenstein argued, people who can communicate have reached agreement on a way of life, which implies the acceptance of common standards. This is not a theme that I shall be able to develop in the present work, so I shall merely state what I think are good reasons for saying that there is always some measure of agreement between people who engage in moral arguments: (a) If people argue about whether something is right or wrong, they are agreeing that it is a moral problem. (b) If they are arguing about its morality on the same grounds (e. g., it is a homicide whose justifiability they are disputing), they are in agreement at least in respect of their formal concepts, which presupposes some positive agreement on substantial matters (e. g., to accept the formal concept of 'murder' as 'unjustifiable homicide' implies the belief that the taking of human life requires a special justification). (c) If they both accept that certain matters are relevant (e. g., if they agree that its 'deterrent value' is relevant to the discussion of the morality of capital punishment) then they are, to that degree, following the same *rationale*. (d) If there are any agreed cases (e. g., this, that and the other are all 'murder') and the argument is about whether or not the questionable case is similar to them in the relevant respects, then there is a great deal of agreement between them.

The problem of finding agreement is most acute when there is a confrontation between different conceptual systems; that is, when people are from different cultural (or sub-cultural) groups. The concepts are formed from different points of view, and there does not seem to be any point of view which would serve as an independent, and common, scale by which to measure the two. It is for this reason that D. Z. Phillips and H. O. Mounce argue in *Moral Practices* (a book which defends a position similar in many other respects to that of the present work) that moral disagreements are undecidable.

Of the many illuminating examples which Phillips and Mounce use to support their arguments, I shall discuss three which have special relevance to the point in question. (a) In an incisive discussion of Abraham's intended sacrifice of Isaac, the authors show that, because of the differences in cultural background (especially with respect to the practice of child-sacrifice), it would be logically impossible for someone in our society to perform the *same act*, even if he were to go through the same physical motions. They explain, in an analysis which is similar to mine, how the ancients would have distinguished child-sacrifice from murder and they warn us against the temptation of saying 'that *really* murder is being committed . . . no matter what the people concerned might say'. Although we might want to condemn such practices from our own point of view, we must beware of any attempt to reduce moral practices to the artificial unity of a single form.[37] (b) A 'scientific rationalist' is arguing with a Roman Catholic housewife about birth control: 'For the rationalist, the possibility of the mother's death or injury, the economic situation of the family, the provision of good facilities for the children, and so on, would be extremely important. The housewife too agrees about providing the good things of life for children, but believes that one ought to begin by allowing them to enter the world. For her, submission to the will of God, the honour of motherhood, the creation of new life, and

so on, are of the greatest importance.' The authors argue that
it is hard to see how these two could reach agreement without
renouncing what they believe in, and conclude that 'there is
no settling of the issue in terms of some supposed common
evidence called human good and harm, since what they differ
over is precisely the question of what constitutes human good
and harm. The same is true of all fundamental moral
disagreements.'[38] (c) Phillips and Mounce recount a story
about an argument between Wittgenstein and Moore as a
'good example of disagreement over the application of the concept of rudeness'. Wittgenstein, in his agitation over a
philosophical problem, kept interrupting Moore before he had
made his point. 'Moore thought that Wittgenstein's behaviour
was rude, holding that good manners should always prevail,
even in philosophical discussion. Wittgenstein, on the other
hand, thought Moore's view of the matter absurd: philosophy
is a serious business, important enough to justify becoming
unmannerly in one's excitement and agitation; to think this
rudeness is simply to misapply the judgment.' The authors
point out correctly that this example shows how 'standards of
rudeness have been influenced by wider beliefs; in other
words, how the judgment, "That is rude", is not entailed by
the facts', but they conclude that it is evidence for 'the possibility of permanent radical moral disagreement'.[39]

Apart from such examples, Phillips and Mounce also have
an argument of principle which is meant to distinguish ethical
differences from other sorts of disagreement:

> The difficulty, however, is to know what these requests
> mean. One understands what is meant if someone asks
> which of two astronomical theories about a star is the cor-
> rect one. But what does one want to know in asking which
> morality is the correct one? In the case of conflicting
> theories about the star, we can imagine, roughly, the sort of
> empirical evidence which might settle the dispute. But
> there is nothing comparable in morality. There is
> something *independent* of the astronomical theories against
> which their validity can be checked, namely, the star in
> question. (Italics mine.)[40]

In other words, since morally neutral facts do not, as such,
enter into ethical inquiry, and since it is only in terms of such

facts that this sort of inquiry could conceivably be settled, ethical disagreements are, in principle, undecidable.

There are three basic mistakes that Phillips and Mounce make which lead them to take the position that ethical disagreements are undecidable: (a) they confuse *de facto* and *de jure* (in principle) differences; (b) they make the false assumption that the only grounds upon which ethical differences *could* be settled would be in terms of factual agreement; (c) they believe that to claim to be able to settle moral differences is to attempt to impose a unique, final moral code.

We saw in the Wittgenstein–Moore story how our authors leaped from a quite ordinary, even pedestrian, misunderstanding to the notion of a 'permanent radical moral disagreement'. Similar examples of the confusion between the *de facto* and the *de jure* are abundant in *Moral Practices*, the most striking being the occasion on which they conclude one paragraph with the statement that 'it is clear that deadlock in ethics will be a common occurrence' and begin the next with the observation that many 'philosophers are not convinced that there need be a breakdown in moral argument'.[41] These statements are certainly not equivalent.

The contretemps which disturbed the friendship of the two great philosophers arose, as our authors acknowledge, because of differences in 'wider beliefs', and it is towards such beliefs that the disputants' attention would have been directed, rather than towards their disparate standards of 'rudeness', had they cared to resolve their differences. There is surely no reason to equate such a minor difficulty with 'permanent, radical disagreement'.

My argument that ethical differences can be settled rationally does not deny that there will be frequent deadlocks in ethics; it simply asserts that there is no reason, in principle, why there *need* be such breakdowns. This obvious distinction between the *de facto* and the *de jure* can be illustrated in arithmetic: Goldbach's conjecture that every even number is the sum of two primes is *undecided* because no one has ever been able to think of any way to prove or disprove it; the Gödelian sentence is *undecidable* in principle. As obvious as the distinction is, Phillips and Mounce are not alone in confusing it.

The discussion of in-principle decidability can be clarified by consideration of the question, whether the only method of solving ethical differences is by factual agreement. Because the Catholic housewife and the scientific rationalist are not in dispute over any facts, Phillips and Mounce contend that their differences are irresoluble, despite the fact that they share an immense background of moral evaluation. After all, many of us have shifted, continue to shift, and maintain uneasy alliances between the two moral standpoints here illustrated; it is at best arbitrary to assert that there are no grounds for rational discussion, that the issue is radically undecidable. (The statement that the housewife and the rationalist could not reach agreement 'without renouncing what they believe in' is merely a truism, emotively stated; there is no realm of discourse in which disagreements, other than those generated by simple factual error, can be settled without someone changing his beliefs.)

It is well known that, for the past few decades, any discussion of the decidability of moral problems has taken place within the context established by the work of C. L. Stevenson. His distinction between matters of 'belief' (i. e., logic and morally neutral fact) and 'attitude' was the basis of his conclusion that ethical differences are in principle interminable. Since, as he thought, it is possible for two people to be in complete agreement in 'belief' but yet differ in 'attitude', there is nothing further for them to produce as evidence and therefore no way for them to settle their difference. This position is central because later writers (although they differ in other respects) presume that the question of decidability (indeed, the question of cognitivity) rests upon the question of whether or not we can derive moral conclusions from morally neutral fact. They are still, on both sides of the naturalistic fence, arguing within the Stevensonian context.

Phillips and Mounce agree with me that this is wrong from the beginning. Morally neutral facts do not enter into moral discourse. The relevance and importance of facts is determined by the conceptual framework within which moral judgements are made. Although some differences in moral judgement may result from factual disagreement, these are comparatively trivial; the philosophically interesting disagreements are those which can be traced to conceptual differences.

My position is that Stevenson's premises are unacceptable; it is not the case that we have recourse only to morally neutral fact when we are trying to settle a moral argument. Since moral differences are chiefly conceptual differences, we ought to seek for conceptual clarification and agreement, and there is no principle which rules out this possibility. Therefore, agreement is attainable in principle. It is, of course, possible to deny that conceptual differences can be resolved, but there are insuperable difficulties attendant upon such a denial. Such a thesis would be claiming that when what is in dispute is not what the facts are, but what the facts amount to, then there can be no good reason for preferring one opinion to another. This would make nonsense, for example, of judicial procedures, and as a philosophical thesis would be self-defeating. Since philosophical differences are pre-eminent examples of conceptual differences, this thesis would assert that there is no good reason why *it* should be accepted.

When they attempt to bolster their position by reference to astronomical theory, Phillips and Mounce allow themselves to be misled by a faulty conception of science. No philosopher of science, except perhaps a few old-line positivists, believes in the possibility of theory-neutral observation statements, and it is generally agreed that Einstein was right when he said: 'Whether you can observe a thing or not depends on the theory which you use. It is the theory which decides what can be observed.'[42] Virtually everything that I have said about the place of facts in moral discourse can be said about experimental evidence in scientific discourse (e. g., we would not know what facts to look for outside a conceptual scheme; the relevance and importance of experimental evidence is determined by the concepts being employed, etc.). There is a fundamental theorem which says that it is always possible to explain any finite set of observations by two incompatible theories; which is to say that there is an indefinite number of possibly correct explanations of any set of facts, or that the probability of any theory is zero. 'Crucial experiments' and 'neutral observation statements' are bits of positivist mythology.

Phillips and Mounce join Stevenson and Hare in their attempt to distinguish ethics from other fields on the basis of the relation of ethical opinions to facts. I certainly do not want to deny that ethics is different, for example, from science, but I do want to insist that you cannot do it *that* way. If you want to say that ethical disagreements are in principle interminable for the reasons which we have been discussing, then you have to say that all disagreements are likewise interminable and you have not succeeded in saying anything distinctive about ethics.

One of the liveliest issues in the philosophy of science has arisen from the confrontation of the opinions of Popper and Kuhn. Without any intention of taking sides in this debate, I should like to quote a statement of Kuhn's which, *mutatis mutandis*, perfectly incapsulates the position which I have been defending. Kuhn argues that, although Popper denies the possibility of theory-neutral observations, his position regarding theory choice nevertheless presumes such observations:

> [Popper] and his followers share with more traditional philosophers of science the assumption that the problem of theory-choice can be resolved by techniques which are semantically neutral. The observational consequences of both theories are first stated in a shared basic vocabulary (not necessarily complete or permanent). Some comparative measure of their truth/falsity count then provides the basis for a choice between them. For Sir Karl and his school, no less than for Carnap and Reichenbach, canons of rationality thus derive exclusively from those of logical and linguistic syntax. Paul Feyerabend provides the exception which proves that rule. Denying the existence of a vocabulary adequate to neutral observation reports, he at once concludes to the intrinsic irrationality of theory-choice.
>
> That conclusion is surely Pickwickian. . . . One can deny . . . the existence of an observation language shared in its entirety by two theories and still hope to preserve good reasons for choosing between them. [43]

Similarly, and finally, one can surely argue that a way of life which does not include the practice of child-sacrifice is preferable to one which does without implying that the preferred moral practice is the one, final and correct form of morality. Einstein did not, after all, claim that the General Theory was the final, complete description of the universe.

Part Three

Conclusions and Speculations

28. *The Conditions and Implications of Consistency*

My arguments could be characterised as a study of the requirements of consistency in ethical judgement. It has been part of my thesis that there are certain conditions which must be satisfied if this requirement is to be met and that, therefore, it is illogical to require consistency and to deny that these conditions can be fulfilled. In the course of this investigation I have made some positive statements about the prerequisites for logical consistency in moral judgement which lead to some conclusions and which open the possibility of further investigations about the nature of moral discourse.

It is a *sine qua non* of judging like cases alike that one be able to tell which cases are alike. This is the function of moral concepts. The two cardinal features which we have discovered about these concepts is that they enable us to recognise similarity among actions from a distinctive, moral point of view and that they are open-textured. Because of these features, the ability to make moral judgements which meet the demands of logical consistency (belief in which ability is implied in the giving of the injunction to judge like cases alike) presupposes that ethics is a rational, or cognitive, activity. This is not to say that there is no more to the rationality of ethics than consistency in moral judgement; it is rather to say that one cannot restrict the rationality of ethics to such consistency. If it is admitted that moral activity is rational in the weak sense, that moral judgements are governed by the logical rule that they be consistent, then it must be admitted that it is rational in the strong sense that moral judgements can be rationally justified.

In what follows I shall expand the compact summary of the last paragraph into four theses about moral discourse. In the first three I shall try to show that the demand for logical consistency in moral judgements is incompatible with a noncognitive view of ethics. In the fourth I shall argue that consistency in moral judgement is not the same as fidelity to specific rules of conduct. This will lead to the consideration of questions which have been raised, rather than answered, by the present inquiry and to some concluding, speculative remarks about the 'basis of ethics'.

29.   Open-Texture and Consistency

To demand logical consistency in moral judgement is to say that someone who makes a moral judgement is logically obliged to judge all similar cases in the same way. However one explains the first judgement, if one requires logical consistency, one must admit that these similar cases are to be decided on the basis of their similarity to the paradigm case (or to the agreed members of the relevant class); there is no room for any other explanation of these judgements. That is to say, if a case is similar to another about which a moral judgement has been made, then one could not consistently hold both (a) that a similar judgement is logically required in the second case; and (b) that the second judgement is a matter of approval or decision.

Because moral terms are open-textured, one does not know the precise extent of one's commitments when making a moral judgement. Since there can be no strict distinction between clear cases (i. e., those which are obviously similar to the paradigm) and unclear cases, the requirement that one judge consistently does not permit one to ignore unclear cases – to draw the line, that is, beyond which one is not committed. If it is questionable whether a case is of a type about which one is morally committed, consistency requires that this question be answered, since it would be inconsistent either to treat the case differently, if it were similar, or to treat it similarly, if it were dissimilar from the moral point of view. This sort of question, we have seen, can be decided by rational means. Therefore, consistency demands that questionable cases be decided on the basis of whether or not they are of the relevant type.

If I am correct in arguing that all moral problems are questions about the extent of the applications of presently held concepts, then all moral judgements are judgements which are made to meet the requirements of consistency. There is no room for a non-cognitive interpretation. This is not to say that theories which explain moral judgements in terms of sentiments, approvals or decisions are self-contradictory. It is to say that the combination of such explanations with a demand for logical consistency is a contradiction.

30. *Consistency and Contradiction*

If there is to be a demand for logical consistency in moral judgements, then there must be a difference between consistency and inconsistency in moral judgements. If two judgements are inconsistent, one could not, without self-contradiction, accept both. Thus, if two people make mutually incompatible moral judgements, a third person could not agree with both of them. Does this imply, as it does in other fields of inquiry, that at least one of the two is mistaken?

In Part One we saw that moral judgements make an interpersonal claim to validity. In order to judge consistently, one must believe that others ought to agree with one's judgements. Universalisability implies, to borrow Polanyi's term, *universal intent*. Thus, if two people make incompatible moral judgements, each is committed to the belief that the other ought to change his mind – which is to say that each believes the other is mistaken. We saw in Part Two that moral differences can be settled by rational means. If agreement is reached, one (or both) of the disputants will have changed his (or their) mind, since the agreed solution cannot be compatible with two mutually incompatible positions. That this is so can be made apparent by supposing that the solution is a position suggested by a third party; and we have seen that a third person cannot consistently agree with both of two incompatible positions. A person who is persuaded by rational argument to accept a solution which is inconsistent with his original position cannot, without self-contradiction, continue to maintain his original position; that is to say, he is committed to the belief that his original position was a mistake.

In general, let us say that someone is mistaken in holding an opinion if he can be brought by rational argument to accept another opinion which is incompatible with the first. If this sense is accepted, then the reply to the query, whether at least one of the two people making incompatible moral judgements is mistaken, is *yes*. In the last paragraph we saw that, when an agreed solution to a moral problem is found, at least one of the disputants is logically committed to the belief that his original position was a mistake. If I am correct in arguing during this inquiry that such agreement can always, in principle, be attained, then at least one of the two people holding incompatible moral opinions can, in principle, be shown to have been mistaken.

One must add the cautionary note that it is not being claimed that there is some simple decision-procedure by which one of two conflicting judgements about the morality of a particular course of action can be shown to be mistaken. In Part Two (section 27) we saw that such a difference in appraisal could belong to one of four problem-types, reflecting different levels of disagreement. To identify the precise area of disagreement and to resolve the dispute on the basis of agreed beliefs is by no means a simple inquiry which will lead to incontestable conclusions about the morality of particular actions. What is being claimed is that one who believes that moral judgements can meet the demands of logical consistency is committed to the belief that moral judgements can be mistaken.

31. *A Matter of Belief*

If it is the case that at least one of two conflicting moral judgements is mistaken, then it would follow that moral differences and agreements are differences and agreements in belief. In this section I seek to show why I think that my arguments substantiate this opinion. In particular, I want to argue that, given complete agreement about morally neutral aspects of a case, if two people disagree in their moral judgements about that case, their disagreement is one of belief.

We saw in Part Two (section 23) that the sense of moral terms provides an objective control for ethical inquiry and that the evidence to support statements about that sense is to be found in the agreed members of the corresponding class of actions. Actions which are of the same type are similar to one another, and the question of what things are similar is a matter of belief. The types of action which are relevant to the making of moral judgements are moral types; that is, the similarity among actions designated by moral terms is such that it can be detected only from the moral point of view. Because a moral judgement is a judgement that certain acts are similar to one another, it is the expression of a belief, and because this similarity is irreducibly moral, it is the expression of a moral belief.

Moral terms operate in the same way as what we may call 'type-words': i. e., the descriptive words of everyday discourse, such as 'red', 'car', 'tree' or 'man', which identify things as being of a certain kind. It is obvious that moral terms perform a special function, that they are concerned with the assessment and guidance of human behaviour; but this is what makes them moral terms and not, say, colour terms or physical-object terms. It is not a logical weakness of a branch of inquiry that its terms classify from a unique point of view or, what amounts to the same thing, that its terms cannot be defined in terms which have been formed from a different point of view. As we have seen (Part One, section 7), if such a definition were possible, it would mean that that branch of inquiry did not have a point of view. When I say that moral terms operate like other type-words, what I mean is that, in both cases, when one has grasped the relevant concepts, one is able to use these words to designate appropriate specimens, and this ability is contingent upon one's ability to recognise the appropriate similarity.

Let us imagine a word, '*fing*', which operates differently. The rule to be followed in the use of '*fing*' is this: Copies of every photograph made in the world are sent to Paris where they are jumbled together in a great box. A blindfolded man spends some time every day picking photographs out of the box; a '*fing*' is anything pictured in the photographs which he picks. We could give '*fing*' a role in a way of life by imagining that prizes are given to anyone who owns a *fing* or finds a *fing*. '*Fing*' differs from ordinary type-words because knowing the rule governing the use of the word would not enable one to recognise *fings* when one encountered them. One could not, for example, learn to use '*fing*' by means of ostensive definition, for even if one knew every present instance of '*fing*' one would not be able to recognise new *fings*. The only way to identify *fings* is to memorise the list of *fings*. This is because *fings* have nothing in common; they are a random collection. The concept of '*fing*' is lacking in intelligibility, not because we cannot understand what a *fing* is (I have said what a *fing* is), but because there is no *rationale* behind the selection procedure; indeed, the point of the rule by which *fings* are selected is precisely that it selects things at random. '*Fing*' is lacking the sort of intelligible sense that ordinary type-words have because *fings* have no common similarity.

In order to use a type-word sensibly, one must know that a given collection of things are similar to one another and understand why they are similar. The second condition is necessary because, for example, if I am told that a, b and c are similar to one another but do not understand why, I will not be able to tell if d is also similar to them; this is the basis for one of the more important devices used in the testing of intelligence. This is one reason why we can follow tacit rules in the use of ordinary words, whereas we would have to follow an explicit procedure in identifying *fings*: the use of ordinary type-words depends upon understanding, and understanding cannot be completely verbalised for the simple reason that these words themselves would have to be understood.

Thus, when a person makes a statement of the form: 'This is X', where X is a type-word, he is expressing the belief that there is a class of things which are similar to one another and that this is one of them. If he did not believe this, he would believe that the word was lacking in intelligibility, like '*fing*', and he could not sensibly use it in this fashion. Therefore, to rely upon a type-word to designate things implies the belief that the corresponding concept correctly classifies things from the appropriate point of view. Since moral terms operate as type-words, this also applies to them. When someone makes a moral judgement (e. g., 'This is murder.'), and even when someone poses a moral problem (e. g., 'I wonder whether this is right; it strikes me that it might be murder.'), he is accepting a moral concept as a valid classification of human actions. He is saying, that is, that there is a class of actions which are similar to one another and that this action is, or he wonders if it is, also similar to them. A moral concept makes an objective claim (to make a correct classification of similar cases), and the acceptance of a moral concept is the belief that this claim is justified. Since moral types cannot be defined in morally neutral terms, moral concepts classify actions which are similar only from the moral point of view, and the belief that such a classification is correct is a moral belief. Furthermore, the belief that people can use moral terms sensibly (which belief is implied in the requirement that moral judgements be consistent) implies the belief that they can recognise similarity from the moral point of view; i. e., that moral opinions are matters of belief.

In any piece of ethical inquiry or argumentation, there are some moral terms whose sense is not in question; they form the frame of reference for the inquiry. It is not, of course, that they are not *questionable* concepts, but they are not at this point *in question*; they are being relied upon in order to question something else. If one of these terms is called into question, then that is a different inquiry (see section 27) which requires different terms of reference, and these terms would then be unquestioned. To rely upon a concept as the unquestioned term of reference in an inquiry implies belief that its claim to classify correctly is justified. Thus, anybody who engages in ethical inquiry, who makes moral judgements and decisions, implicitly believes in the validity of his concepts. When it is a case of moral argument, the terms which the disputants use in common, upon whose sense they agree, represent an area of substantial agreement, so that the conclusion they reach (which, as we saw, is a judgement about the conceptual subsumption of the questionable case) is an agreement in belief. It is true that such agreement can be mistaken, but that is not the point. The point is that it is agreement in belief, not a coincidence of their approvals or decisions.

32. *Consistency and Rules*

I have objected in Part Two (section 22) to the notion that consistency in moral judgement is to be measured by fidelity to rules of conduct. I pointed out that, rather than ensuring consistency, this would involve perpetual self-contradiction. The criterion of consistency, I argued, is the 'sense' of moral judgements. We have seen (section 25) that this 'sense' is the *rationale* of the operative moral concept and that the rules of conduct are the explication of that *rationale*. The latter discussion provides the theoretical basis for explaining why consistency in moral judgement is not to be equated with fidelity to rules of conduct which are framed in morally neutral terms. The discussion of this question will lead to a broader understanding of what is entailed in requiring that moral judgements be logically consistent and will bring to light some problems which the present inquiry will leave unsolved.

There are four reasons for saying that we must look beyond rules of conduct in order to find the criterion of consistency in moral judgement:

(1)   Since rules of conduct are open-textured, consistency requires that we be able to decide the unavoidable questionable cases. This obviously cannot be accomplished by an inspection of the rule or by a resolution to apply the rule consistently. It is because the rule is not clear about this case that it is a questionable case. As we have seen, such questions are decided by reference to the *rationale* behind the rule.

(2)   The explication of a moral concept into rules of conduct is never complete and final. A change in historical circumstances or a deeper understanding of the concept could require that there be further clarifications and, perhaps, new explications. After any change in a rule of conduct (e. g., in making an exception) there is a formal contradiction between the modified rule and the original. If logical consistency in moral judgement were to be found at the level of rules of conduct, every modification of these rules would violate the logical rule requiring consistency. However, such modifications are made in the name of consistency. If they were not made, the rigidly adhered-to rules would be *inconsistent* with the *rationale* of which they are supposed to be the ex-

plication. Consistency at the lower level is maintained at the cost of consistency at the higher, yet it is the higher level (i. e., the *rationale*) which gives sense to the lower. Without the *rationale* one would not be able to apply the rules consistently. The requirement of logical consistency in moral judgement is met by consistency in the exercise of moral concepts, not by fidelity to rules of conduct. Such fidelity is, of course, generally required as well, since such rules are warranted because they are explications of moral concepts, but consistency sometimes demands that the rules be changed or broken.

The fact that rules of conduct function as the explication of moral concepts (if, that is, I am correct in thinking that it is a fact) has, as has been mentioned, an obvious relevance to the question of ethical relativism (of which I shall say a little more below) and to the related question of the possibility of framing exceptionless rules. I. M. Crombie, for example, notes that one does not hesitate to say that such things as 'murder', 'cruelty' or 'lying' are always wrong, but that one does hesitate to say this of some morally neutral action-type:

> . . . I have no hesitation in saying that one ought never to do a cruel act, simply because I know that if I come across some case of severity, which I know to be extreme but believe to be necessary, I can and shall withhold the description 'cruelty' from it. I hesitate to say that one ought never to tell a deliberate falsehood because I hesitate to give away in advance my right to approve of doing what would be unquestionably just this in some situation which might conceivably arise.[1]

My analysis of moral concepts explains this; we cannot frame exceptionless moral rules in morally neutral terms because of the open-texture of moral terms. I hardly need add that the reservation of the right to refuse to apply moral terms to cases which one does not want to condemn – as Crombie vividly puts it: 'So long as I am allowed to boggle over *whether* the cap fits, I need not hesitate to condemn *whatever* the cap fits'[2] – is not to retreat from moral responsibility; it is to claim moral responsibility, for it is to say that the application of a moral term is a moral judgement. It is the attempt to define moral terms in morally neutral terms which threatens the notion of moral responsibility, since it amounts to a denial that there is a moral point of view.

The recognition that consistency in moral judgement is to be measured in reference to the *rationale* helps us to interpret historical development in morality as a constant striving for consistency in the exercise of moral concepts. We shall now see how this striving for consistency reaches beyond one moral concept into a wider range of the conceptual scheme.

(3) Consistency in moral judgement cannot mean fidelity to rules of conduct because it is always possible to think of situations in which two such rules conflict. If consistency required fidelity to these rules, then one would be faced with the anomaly of a logical rule prescribing its own contradiction. If one is to achieve consistency of judgement in these situations, one must clarify the relevant concepts and the relations among them sufficiently to allow one to resolve the apparent contradiction. If there is a real contradiction, it would mean that there is a mistaken belief which has been incorporated into the conceptual scheme and that this must be corrected if consistency in moral judgement is to be achieved.

(4) Consistency in moral judgement cannot mean fidelity to rules of conduct because it can happen that a change in a non-moral, but relevant, belief is such that fidelity to certain rules becomes an inconsistency. For example, if a Christian becomes a Hindu, or a believer becomes an unbeliever, he can no longer, with logical consistency, remain faithful to the rules of conduct by which he had explicated his concept of sacrilege. A change of belief about what is sacred requires the enunciation of new rules or, in the second instance, the abrogation of all rules of conduct with regard to the treatment of sacred things.

Since consistency in the use of moral terms is a function of the *rationale* governing the use of these terms, and since this *rationale* is contingent upon some relevant, non-moral beliefs, consistency in moral judgement is also contingent upon these beliefs. If, as was suggested above, we can explain ethical development as the result of the striving for consistency in the exercise of moral concepts, we might plausibly define morality as the striving for consistency between our knowing and our doing.

33. *Moral and Non-Moral Beliefs*

These considerations have led us from the firm ground of reasonably (and, one hopes, correctly) argued conclusions to rather more tenuous speculations. Once we have broken the hold over our attention that has been exercised by rules of conduct (as I hope that the arguments of this study have helped to do), and gone beyond these rules to the *rationale* that makes them sensible, we are, on the one hand, equipped to deal with difficulties which appeared to be insurmountable before this conceptual shift; but, on the other hand, our new position poses problems of its own which require further speculation and new arguments.

The chief difficulty that attaches to my position (or so it seems to me) is to state the precise relationship which obtains between moral concepts and the relevant, non-moral beliefs upon which they depend. This is not a problem which I shall even try to solve. I shall, however, try to state some aspects of the problem and to offer a few speculations about what directions a further inquiry might take.

Let me say, at first, that I do not think it can seriously be doubted that there is a logical relation between moral beliefs and relevant, non-moral beliefs. We have already seen how the *rationale* governing the use of 'sacrilege', 'murder' and 'lie' is dependent upon certain non-moral beliefs. In addition, one thinks readily of the example of the tribe in which it was the obligation of children to kill their parents at an early age because of the belief that people lived for ever in the stage of physical development at which they died.[3] One thinks also of the arguments that B. G. Mitchell has offered to show that differences of opinion about the rightness of legal enforcement of morality can be traced to differences in metaphysical belief.[4] In all such cases, the explication of moral concepts into rules of conduct is dependent upon relevant, non-moral beliefs. The relationship is logical because the adherence to rules of conduct which resulted from an explication of the moral concept prior to the change in a relevant belief can involve one in contradiction. That this is the case is not apparent if one attends only to the fact that rules of conduct are 'ought' statements and that there is a logical gap between these and the 'is' statements in which one states the relevant non-moral beliefs. It would appear that, logically, one could make any 'ought' statement without thereby contradicting an 'is' statement. However, this is something like saying that one could make a table out of air. As we have noted, there is a logical gap between the teleological definition of 'table' and the observable properties that go to make up tables. But this obviously does not mean that *anything* can be a table. The *rationale* of 'table' establishes standards that must be met if an object is to count as a table. It is similar with moral concepts. Rules of conduct are the explication of moral concepts; as such they are logically dependent upon the corresponding *rationale*. The criterion of consistency in moral judgement is the *rationale*, not the explication, and the *rationale* changes with a change in relevant, non-moral beliefs. Therefore, adherence to a rule of conduct which was the result of the explication of the unmodified concept could lead to contradiction. For example, to treat an object with special reverence for the reason that it is sacred implies the belief that the object is sacred. If one now believes that nothing is sacred, one is, in following the rule of conduct, involved in self-contradiction.

To say that there is a logical relationship between moral beliefs and relevant non-moral beliefs is to pose a problem, not to offer an explanation. There is a great deal that needs to be worked out before one could describe the precise nature of this relationship, at least as much work as it took us to get to this point of posing the problem within a suitable context. However, insofar as it is a *logical* problem it does not seem to be a problem that is peculiar to ethics. We have seen that, given a moral term, questions of relevance are settled by reference to the *rationale* which governs the use of that term; that is, the problem is a particular instance of the general logical problem about the relation between the meaning of a term and the extensional criteria which are the explication of that meaning. Although it might appear that it is the 'inductive' question – how is it that we develop moral concepts – which is particularly pressing, this too is a problem which is every bit as difficult in any other universe of discourse. There may well be, in this regard, special problems about the validation of ethical concepts, but since the immediately apparent distinctive feature of ethics is its subject-matter and the point of view from which it treats this subject-matter, the correct procedure would seem to be to search for a method of validating this type of concept rather than treating ethics as if it were, for example, a species of sense perception and finding it, understandably, deficient in this respect.

It is a general characteristic of type-words that there is a, not completely specifiable, *rationale* which underlies their use. This *rationale* is the norm for the assessment of correct use in particular instances, but if the validity of the concept is in question, the *rationale* becomes itself the subject of inquiry. Thus: (a) The notion of a conceptual *rationale* does not belong to ethical theory; it highlights that aspect of the more complex notion of 'meaning' which has been relevant to the present discussion. (b) A necessary step in an investigation of the validity of ethical concepts is a study of the *rationale* behind the use of moral terms. As we have seen, there are good reasons to think that such an investigation will not be easily prosecuted. In the first place, there are both social and objective influences upon the conceptual *rationale* and one or the other of these factors predominates in different types of term. For example, a word like 'tree' which designates a natural class of objects is less subject to social influence than is a word like 'table' which, as Kovesi has shown, is strongly bound up with cultural conditions. This is so because 'table' is not only formed within a way of life, as are all words, but the things it designates are also so formed. Moral terms are further along this continuum since they are both formed within ways of life and are themselves constitutive of ways of life. Secondly, since the *rationale* behind the use of a word like 'murder' is dependent upon such a wide range of beliefs, the analysis of this *rationale* would seem to set a more difficult task than would be the case with, say, physical-object words.

One can form some expectations of what an analysis of the *rationale* of a moral term like 'murder' would reveal. One would expect to find, for example, that the notion rested upon a combination of more basic moral beliefs together with some relevant non-moral beliefs, since a person who thinks that the taking of human life requires a special justification must hold some non-moral beliefs about the distinctiveness of man as well as a moral standard which dictates that these distinguishing features entitle man to special consideration. One could conjecture, further, that with respect to any non-moral belief there is a more basic ethical notion which determines this belief's relevance. For example, we know that belief in the fact that capital punishment deters crime is part of the *rationale* of some people's moral standards about capital punishment; but we have seen that the relevance of this non-moral belief is dependent upon a moral belief. The reason to believe that this relationship will hold no matter how deeply one probes the concept of murder is the principle that morally neutral facts *qua* morally neutral do not suggest moral problems.

One important consequence of the mixed nature of a moral term's *rationale* is its relevance to ethical differences and, more broadly, to the question of ethical relativism. Let us consider the opinions of four people with regard to capital punishment: A believes that it is justified because it is a deterrent to crime; B believes that capital punishment does not deter crime but that, if it did, it would be justified; C believes that the State is never justified in taking someone's life; D believes that capital punishment is justified on purely retributive grounds. A and D share the opinion that capital punishment is morally justified; B and C agree in condemning it. However, it is A and B whose moral outlooks are similar; their different moral standards with regard to capital punishment can be traced to a factual disagreement. Similarly, people who believed that one ought to kill one's parents when they reach the age of fifty might appear to have moral notions which are radically different from our own; but if this rule is based on a non-moral belief about life after death, there might be no basic difference in moral belief.

The question that naturally suggests itself at this point is what we should find if we were to trace the roots of moral concepts back to the very beginning. What sort of beliefs are at the foundation of moral thought? Since this is a question which requires a great deal more study – ethical, logical and epistemological – any opinion offered at this stage would be premature and ill-considered. Fortunately, the conclusions which we have reached concerning the cognitivity of ethics and the logical structure of moral concepts and arguments do not require that this question be answered, but rather set the context within which it can sensibly be asked.

Negatively, one might point out that there are reasons to make one doubt whether the project of finding a set of ultimate moral beliefs can be successfully carried out: (a) The belief that there must be a set of such rock-bottom propositions seems to be akin to the discredited theory of logical atomism. (b) The belief that there must be a set of axioms which provide the ultimate justification for all the statements made within a given system of thought is true if, and only if, all human thought can be construed on the model of a deductive system like Euclid's geometry. Perhaps one would be permitted to maintain a sceptical reserve with regard to this proposition until such time as the natural sciences have received a similar formalisation.

34. *The Moral Point of View and the Basis of Ethics*

One conclusion which was reached and which will no doubt be useful in a further analysis of moral concepts is that there is a distinctive moral point of view. Since the existence of such a point of view was inferred from the way we use moral terms, and since no further arguments turned on a description of it, we have had no occasion to say any more than that there is a moral point of view and that it is distinctive. However, the arguments that have led us to conclude that there is such a point of view also give us some idea of what it is like.

The first thing to recall is that what is distinctive about the moral point of view is not that it is a *point of view* but that it is *moral*. The expression 'point of view', as it has been used in this study, has carried no special theoretical burdens; it has been used in its everyday sense. In visual perception, one sees different things from different points of view, since even the same objects are seen from different angles; similarly, one understands things differently from different conceptual points of view, since different aspects of things become relevant considerations and different similarities between things are detected. Our conclusion that there is a distinctive moral point of view has followed from our recognition of the fact that moral terms designate types of action which cannot be described in morally neutral terms; that is, it is a necessary condition of the way we use moral terms that these terms be formed from a distinctive point of view.

The reason that no morally neutral description will denote all and only those things denoted by a term like 'murder' is that what is to count as an action of a moral type is determined by a standard for assessing the value of the reason for which the action is performed. It is central to the moral point of view that the performance of certain types of action require a special justification, and although these are neutral types (e. g., homicide), no morally neutral distinction will discriminate those members of the corresponding class which are of a moral type (e. g., murder) from the remainder. Thus moral standards are not expressed in such sentences as 'Smoking is forbidden' in which some imperative, or imperative-like, label is attached to an independently identifiable type of action, but are more like logical statements which assess the relative strength of arguments. The moral point of view, then, consists partly of standards for the assessment of what will justify the performance of certain kinds of action.

It might appear that, since the moral terms we have been studying have to do with actions which are injurious or harmful, this might be a way to supply a morally neutral content to the moral point of view – allowing, of course, for due modifications to account for the positive dictates of morality. There are two senses in which this might be taken: either the morally neutral content is *eo ipso* morally relevant, prior to any moral judgement, or its relevance is dependent upon moral judgement. There are good reasons to think that the first alternative is unacceptable: (a) Although it would be difficult to imagine anyone saying that the performance of certain actions, such as killing a person, was not injurious, there are some things which are considered as injuries as a consequence of moral judgement; for example, it is only in our time that it has been thought that to treat people as unequal is to injure them. 'Injury', that is to say, appears to be a covert moral term. It is plausible to suppose that the sort of action which we think to be injurious regardless of moral considerations might simply be the sort about which our moral opinions are so secure that we never question them. (b) Assessment of actions from the moral point of view requires that there be moral judgements about what is more and less harmful. An Inquisitor's standards in this respect would, for example, be quite different from those of a liberal utilitarian. (c) What is essential to judgements made from the moral point of view is not simply whether the action is harmful but whether the reason for performing the action is sufficient to justify it. (d) That moral judgements are concerned with injurious actions is a consequence of the moral judgement that doing what is harmful requires a special justification.

In a sophisticated version of naturalism G. J. Warnock has tried to specify the content of morality by means of a moderately Hobbesian account of how human affairs tend to go badly.[5] Morality has the ameliorative function of overcoming our 'limited sympathies', and Warnock employs this function to generate some basic moral principles by means of which moral problems can definitely be settled. However, we have learned, under Moore's tutelage, to inquire of any naturalistic theory whether it can be significantly asked if that which is described as 'good' is *really* good. Warnock replies with commendable consistency: 'Yes, you can ask that, but the answer is *no!*' In other words, it is possible to be right, *justifiably* right, in doing what is morally wrong. But surely what we mean by saying that something is *morally* wrong is that it is *categorically* wrong. It is cold comfort to be assured that one can rationally settle moral problems and then to be told that one's conclusions do not say what ought to be done.

The chief reason why Warnock has come to this unpalatable conclusion is that a question about the 'content' of morality (about what sorts of behaviour raise moral issues) is itself a moral question. For example, many questions about sexual behaviour would not be moral questions on Warnock's account. Perhaps they are not, but *whether* they are or not is a moral question. Hareian formalism is doubtless a very good thing to avoid, but this is not properly done by replacing morality with a kind of racial prudence which itself raises authentic moral problems.

The relation between morally neutral content and the moral point of view would appear to be the same as the relation between morally neutral descriptions of murderous acts and the concept of murder. This is not a conclusion that one could insist upon without a great deal more study, but it is what one could expect considering what has been said about moral concepts. If, in the end, the moral point of view could be reduced to a set of morally neutral concepts, it would be difficult to understand how the moral concepts could have developed their autonomous, cognitive, nature – which nature, it will be recalled, was evidence for, not a consequence of, saying that there is a moral point of view.

A more complete description of the moral point of view must wait upon a study of a wider range of moral concepts. One would have to study, for example, virtues and moral ideals, both in themselves and in relation to the action-concepts which we have been considering, before one could claim to offer an adequate theory of morals. One would also have to settle some difficult logical and epistemological problems – especially those concerning the validation of concepts, and the embedding of the moral concepts in their cultural framework – before one could confidently describe the cognitive activity which is characteristic of ethical thought.

References

Preface

1. A. N. Prior, *Logic and the Basis of Ethics* (New York: Oxford University Press, 1949) p. *viii*.
2. Julius Kovesi, *Moral Notions* (London: Routledge, 1967) p. 64.
3. Ibid., p. 65.
4. Michael Polanyi, 'The Message of the Hungarian Revolution', *American Scholar*, XXXV (1966) 261–76; reprinted in Michael Polanyi, *Knowing and Being*, edited by Marjorie Grene (London: Routledge, 1969) p. 33.
5   J. R. Lucas, 'The Lesbian Rule', *Philosophy*, XXX (1955) 109ff.; H. L. A. Hart, *The Concept of Law* (Oxford: Clarendon Press, 1961); Kovesi, op. cit.

Part One: Understanding and Validity in Moral Judgement

1. J. Kemp, *Reason, Action and Morality* (London: Routledge, 1964) pp. 160–1.
2. R. M. Hare, *Freedom and Reason* (Oxford: Clarendon Press, 1963) p. 29.
3. Polanyi, *Personal Knowledge* (London: Routledge, 1958) p. 175.
4. Ibid.
5. Ibid.
6. Anthony Kenny, *Action, Emotion and Will* (London: Routledge, 1963) pp. 189ff.
7. Polanyi, *Personal Knowledge*, p. 175.
8. David Hume, *A Treatise of Human Nature*, ed. L. A. Selby-Bigge (Oxford: Clarendon Press, 1888; reprinted 1951) p. 469.
9. J. R. Searle, *Speech Acts* (Cambridge: University Press, 1969) p. 175.
10. Prior, op. cit., p. 8.
11. Kemp, op. cit., p. 59.
12. A. J. Ayer, *Language, Truth and Logic* (London: Gollancz, 1938).
13. Cf. T. S. Kuhn, *The Structure of Scientific Revolutions* (Chicago: University Press, 1962); Polanyi, 'The Creative Imagination', *Chemical and Engineering News*, XLIV (1966) 85–93.
14. Imre Lakatos, 'Criticism and the Methodology of Scientific Research Programmes', *Proceedings of the Aristotelian Society*, XLIII (1969) 149–86.
15. Ibid., 155–6.
16. Ibid., 156.

17. Ibid., 162.
18. For studies of the philosophical implications of Gödel's theorem, see: J. N. Findlay, Gödelian Sentences: A Non-Numerical Approach', *Mind*, LI (1942) 259–65, reprinted in Findlay's *Language, Mind and Value* (London: Allen and Unwin, 1963); and E Nagel and J. R. Newman, *Gödel's Proof* (London: Routledge, 1959).
19. Hare, op. cit., p. 29.
20. J. A. Passmore, 'The Objectivity of History', *Philosophy*, XXXIII (1958) 106.
21. Ibid.
22. William Whewell, *Philosophy of Discovery* (London, 1860) p. 254.
23. Cf. Kuhn, op. cit.; Polanyi, opera cit.; C. F. A. Pantin, *The Relations Between the Sciences* (Cambridge: University Press, 1969); and Stephen Toulmin, *The Philosophy of Science* (London: Hutchinson, 1953).
24. Cf. Polanyi, *Personal Knowledge*, p. 10 n.
25. Alasdair MacIntyre, *A Short History of Ethics* (New York: Macmillan, 1966) p. 259.
26. Iris Murdoch, 'Vision and Choice in Morality', *Proceedings of the Aristotelian Society*, Suppl. XXX (1956); reprinted in I. T. Ramsey (ed.), *Christian Ethics and Contemporary Philosophy* (New York: Macmillan, 1966) pp. 197–8.
27. D. P. Gauthier, *Practical Reasoning* (Oxford: Clarendon Press, 1963) pp. 4–5.
28. R. M. Hare, *The Language of Morals* (Oxford: University Press, 1973) p. 129.
29. Eric D'Arcy, *Human Acts* (Oxford: Clarendon Press, 1963) p. 25.
30. Plato, *Republic*, 354.
31. Plato, *Meno*, 79.
32. Plato, *Republic*, 336.
33. W. Quine, 'Two Dogmas of Empiricism', *Philosophical Review*, LXV (1951); reprinted in Quine, *From a Logical Point of View* (Cambridge, Mass.: Harvard University Press, 1953).
34. Searle, *Speech Acts*, p. 5.
35. Ibid., p. 6.
36. Ibid.
37. Ibid., pp. 6–7.
38. Ibid., p. 7.
39. B. Rundle, 'Modality and Quantification', in J. R. Butler (ed.), *Analytical Philosophy* (Oxford: Blackwell, 1965).
40. Ibid., p. 38.
41. F. Waismann, 'Verifiability', *Proceedings of the Aristotelian Society*, Suppl. XIX (1945); reprinted in A. G. N. Flew (ed.), *Logic and Language* (Oxford: Blackwell, 1963) vol. I, pp. 117–44.
42. Plato, *Republic*, 331.
43. Ibid., 336.
44. Kovesi, op. cit., pp. 3ff.
45. Hare, *Freedom and Reason*, pp. 21ff. and *passim*.
46. Ibid., p. 22.

47.   Ibid., pp. 22–3.
48.   Ibid., p. 23.
49.   Prior, op. cit., p. *viii*.
50.   Searle, op. cit., p. 8.
51.   A. Tarski, 'The Semantic Conception of Truth and the Foundations of Semantics', *Philosophy and Phenomenological Research*, 1 V (1944) 341–76.
52.   P. T. Geach, *Mental Acts* (London: Routledge, 1957) p. 12.
53.   Cf. Joseph Fletcher, *Situation Ethics* (Philadelphia: Westminster Press, 1966), esp. pp. 74–5. For a discussion of Fletcher's use of this technique, see Paul Ramsey, *Deeds and Rules in Christian Ethics* (New York: Scribner's Sons, 1967) pp. 192ff.
54.   Ramsey, op. cit., ch. 2
55.   K. R. Popper, *Conjectures and Refutations* (London: Routledge, 1963) p. 390.
56.   Polanyi, *Personal Knowledge*, pp. 249–51.
57.   Ibid., esp. ch. 9.
58.   Polanyi, *The Tacit Dimension* (New York: Doubleday, 1966) p. 78.
59.   Passmore, 'Objectivity of History', 108.
60.   Ibid., 109.
61.   Ibid.
62.   Jean-Paul Sartre, *Existentialism and Humanism*, trans. P. Mairet (London: Methuen, 1948) pp. 35–6.
63.   Kemp, *Reason, Action and Morality*, p. 19.
64.   Ibid.
65.   Kovesi, *Moral Notions*, pp. 107–8.

Part Two: The Method of Ethical Inquiry

1.   Ayer, *Language, Truth and Logic*.
2.   Lucas, 'Lesbian Rule', 199.
3.   Ibid., 200.
4.   Passmore, 'Objectivity of History', 109.
5.   Ibid.
6.   D. Pole, *Rational Enquiry* (London: Athlone Press, 1961) p. 86.
7.   For the distinction between a 'rigid' and a 'flexible' framework, see Polanyi, *Personal Knowledge*, pp. 104ff.
8.   Lucas, 'Lesbian Rule', 206ff.
9.   Ibid., 202–3.
10.   Ibid., 205.
11.   Ibid.
12.   Ibid., 206.
13.   Ibid.
14.   Ibid., 207.
15.   Ibid., 208.
16.   Ibid., 211.
17.   Ibid.
18.   Waismann, 'Verifiability', 117–44.
19.   Ibid., 120.

20. Pole, op. cit., pp. 88–9.
21. L. Wittgenstein, *Philosphical Investigations*, trans G. E. M. Anscombe (Oxford: Blackwell, 1963) pp. 31ff.
22. Kovesi, *Moral Notions*, p. 3.
23. Ibid., p. 5.
24. Ibid., pp. 14–15.
25. Ibid., p. 3.
26. Ibid., p. 10.
27. Ibid., pp. 7ff.
28. Hart, *Concept of Law*, pp. 123–4.
29. Ibid., p. 125.
30. Ibid., pp. 125–6.
31. Ibid., p. 126.
32. Ibid., pp. 124ff.
33. Hare, *Freedom and Reason*, p. 8.
34. Ibid., p. 11.
35. Ibid., p. 15.
36. William James, *Principles of Psychology* (1890; reprinted New York: Dover, 1950) vol. I I, p. 110.
37. D. Z. Phillips and H. O. Mounce, *Moral Practices* (London: Routledge, 1970) pp. 109ff.
38. Ibid., pp. 58ff.
39. Ibid., pp. 50ff.
40. Ibid., pp. 104ff.
41. Ibid., p. 54.
42. Quoted in W. Heisenberg, 'Theory, Criticism and a Philosopher', in *From a Life of Physics*, special supplement of the *Bulletin of the International Atomic Energy Agency* (Vienna, 1970) 36ff.
43. T. S. Kuhn, 'Reflections on My Critics', in I. Lakatos and A. Musgrave (eds), *Criticism and the Growth of Knowledge* (Cambridge: University Press, 1970) pp. 234ff.

Part Three: Conclusions and Speculations

1. I. M. Crombie, 'Moral Principles', in I. T. Ramsey (ed.), *Christian Ethics and Contemporary Philosophy*, p. 249.
2. Ibid., p. 249.
3. Cf. W. K. Frankena, *Ethics* (Englewood Cliffs, N. J.: Prentice-Hall, 1963) p. 92.
4. B. G. Mitchell, *Law, Morality and Religion in a Secular Society* (London: Oxford University Press, 1967) pp. 87–102.
5. G. J. Warnock, *The Object of Morality* (London: Methuen, 1970).